No More Mr Nice Guy

SAF Publishing Ltd

No More Mr Nice Guy

The inside story of the Alice Cooper group

Michael Bruce

with Billy James

SAF Publishing Ltd

SAF Publishing Ltd

First published in 1996 by SAF Publishing Ltd.
Revised and updated 2000

SAF Publishing Ltd.
Unit 7, Shaftesbury Centre,
85 Barlby Road,
London W10 6BN
England
Tel: +44 (0)20 8969 6099
Fax: +44 (0)20 8969 6120

www.safpublishing.com

ISBN 0 946719 32 2

Printed in England by Cromwell Press, Trowbridge, Wiltshire.

To my wonderful children; Tyler, Mikaela and Chandler.

Thanks for all the love.

Acknowledgements

Extra special thanks to Billy James, without whose efforts this book would not have been possible. And to my good friends and fellow players and artists, Steve Escallier, Mark Adams, Ed and Marie Ravencrofts, Don Demarest, Tom Michaels, Mike Pileggi at Western.

Thanks to Charlotte & Keith James, Bill Risoli, Gary Brown, Paul Brenton, Bruce Cameron, Andy Long, Skinny Noschka, JK Loftin, Jeff Jatras, Ronnie Newman, Mike Taylor, Tony Grifasi, David Tedds, Jeff Clayton, Dee Clayton, Steve Hallbery, Dave Hallbery, Wayne Langston, Pat Ogelvie, Pete Radloff, Neal Smith, John Wilson.

A very special thank you to John Beaver and John Wilson who both offered archive material without recompense but as a service to their all time favourite band.

Thanks to Joel Levicke for the drawing on page 10.

Addresses

Write to Michael Bruce at:
Wett Blanket Inc, 9901 Richmond Ave, #429, Houston, TX 77042

For more information on ex-Alice Cooper group members and Ant-Bee, please write to:
Glass Onyon, PO Box 207, Carolina Beach, NC 28428-0207. USA

Record companies:
Divine Records, PO Box 775, London E5 9DE, UK
SPV/Rebel Records - Brusseler Strasse 14, 30539, Hannover, Germany
Baloney Shrapnel Records, PO Box 6504, Phoenix, AZ 85005 6504, USA
One Way Records, 15 Industrial Pk Rd, Albany, NY 12206, USA

Websites

email: michaelobruce@aol.com
Official Michael Bruce Site: www.michaelbruceofalicecooper.com
http://hometown.aol.com/michaelobruce/myhomepage/index.html
www.MichaelBruce.com

ANT-BEE Web Bizarre -
http://ourworld.compuserve.com/homepages/antbee/
Official Neal Smith site - www.NealSmith.com
Bruce Cameron Music - www.BruceCameronMusic.com

Contents

Foreword

When I was 12 years old, my favourite band was the Alice Cooper group. There was nothing like them. Hated by parents, they had everything an adolescent boy could get off on — sex, violence, rock 'n' roll, snakes, you name it — hey, I even joined the fan club in 1972. The Alice Cooper group were unique because, not only did they have all the theatrics of a horror movie, but they also wrote some really great tunes. These are songs that have stood the test of time — I mean, everyday somewhere around the world "I'm Eighteen", "School's Out" or "No More Mr Nice Guy" gets played on the radio. One name is consistent in the songwriting department on those original Alice Cooper records and that's Michael Bruce — teen idol of the group. Michael had a real grip on what the kids of the day were into musically and otherwise. His lyrics said something to the kids (and still do).

Recently I had the pleasure of recording and working with Michael on one of my Ant-Bee albums, along with gigging in his Billion Dollar Babies band. You can jam with a million musicians on those old Cooper songs and it still will never sound or feel like it does when you play them with the guy who wrote them! This book was written for all the Alice Cooper group freaks worldwide (you know who you are). It concentrates on the history of the band and Michael Bruce's subsequent solo career. It gives you a scoop on what really went on during Queen Alice's reign. With some of the rarest photos from Michael's personal collection (you should see his scrapbook!), it captures in Michael Bruce's own words, the story of the Alice Cooper group and all their glory. I hope you'll love it to death.

Billy James
co-Author, North Carolina.

Drawing: Joel Levicke

Introduction

Well, what do you remember about the original Alice Cooper group? Yeah, you know, that bunch of weirdos — those sickos who supposedly dismembered chickens, or ripped baby dolls apart. Or maybe you just remember that snake, or the mock hangings, the menacing black eye make-up. Oh yes, and perhaps you remember the great tunes too.

I remember it all. Difficult as this is to believe — I got into the Alice Cooper group in 1971 because of Andy, my five year old brother. Back then I liked to think I was a cool, hip fifteen year old, hooked on Cream, Zeppelin and the Grateful Dead. It was getting to the point where no LP track could be worth its salt if it didn't last the side of an album. The house was full of the sound of "serious" progressive music which blasted permanently from my tinny bedroom stereo, while I struggled to strum along on my first electric guitar.

Envious of my growing collection of vinyl delights, Andy was convinced he wanted an LP for his fifth birthday. So I guided him toward the local record shop to spend his birthday money, hoping I might tempt him with something to my liking. But for some reason he took a fancy to an album with a snake's head on the cover. Obviously I had heard of the Alice Cooper group, but to my purist eyes they weren't exactly serious. I mean, come on, real bands did not wear gold lurex trousers, heavy eye make-up and carry out blood-spattered executions while playing what amounted to pop songs.

Rock credibility aside, I have to admit I was more concerned as to what my mother would say when I returned home with what was little more than a toddler clutching an album by the sickest band imaginable. After the spectacular tantrums that broke out when she tried to part him from his favourite birthday present, he was reluctantly allowed to keep *Killer*. But secretly, I was just a teensy bit jealous. Whilst I had a record collection which my parents considered loud, unlistenable or just plain stupid, my darling little five year old brother had usurped my position as the enfant terrible of the household, by owning a record by a band who were downright dangerous!

In England, the tabloid press had enjoyed a field day reporting Alice's outrageous on-stage antics. In typical style, they loved exaggerating the band's apparent ability to corrupt the youth of a nation! The result was that concerned parents and politicians were attempting to gain an injunction on the group even setting foot on England's green and pleasant land.

Back at home, my parents were more prepared to believe the newspapers than my claims that it was all a piece of harmless fun. They were even more horrified when over the next week or so, Andy, armed with my tennis racket, some knitting needles and biscuit tins, could perform the whole album note-for-note, giving perfect mimed renditions of "Dead Babies" and "Be My Lover" whenever family friends or relatives came round.

He must have played that album 1,000 times in six months and very soon I found myself humming some of the songs on the way to school. The next year, my schoolfriends and I found ourselves down the front at the Wembley Arena shouting for an encore after Alice had not only beaten the injunction, but miraculously survived another night at the gallows!

The group's progress from Arizona, the place of real life Western hangings, to filling 10,000 seater arenas had been an often tortuous and fraught journey. Like most bands of their era, it had all started when a bunch of long-hairs got together at their high school in Phoenix. Like many of their teenage counterparts they had watched in awe as the British invasion of The Beatles and The Stones swept across America, swiftly followed by The Who and The Yardbirds.

After gaining local notoriety as The Earwigs and then The Spiders — creepy crawlies were much in vogue — they upped and moved to LA and changed their name to Alice Cooper, a moniker which embraced the group as a whole, not merely their lead singer. Confusing to many — I mean, where the hell was this girl called Alice Cooper? — the name did little to indicate the future direction of the band. Early material attempted to mix Beatle-influenced melodies, Stones-like sexual pout and Floydian psychedelia, with an increasingly outrageous stage show.

Although they immersed themselves in the late sixties rock 'n' roll scene in LA, hanging out with Jim Morrison, Arthur Lee and all, they found they were often at odds with the prevailing hippie mood of the times. The band's interest in shock theatrics meant their show had violent overtones that made West Coast hippie audiences feel distinctly uncomfortable. LA had produced its fair share of psychedelic mavericks like The Doors, Captain Beefheart and Frank Zappa — but they weren't quite ready for the confrontation of Alice Cooper.

It was in Zappa, that the band found their first champion. Initially he liked what he saw in the Alice Cooper group — essentially a band that could clear a hall in ten minutes — and he signed them to his own Straight label.

It was perhaps appropriate that the band's first LP should be released in 1969, the year when Altamont and Manson ensured that the cream at the top of the "peace and love" sixties went sour. All of a sudden the hippie bands with their talk of revolution and flower power seemed quaint and utopian. There was a feeling that the upcoming generation of kids no longer wanted long spaced-out blues jams — they wanted to be entertained. The sight of endless groups shuffling apologetically on stage in their jeans and T-shirts was getting boring — you might as well have watched the roadies playing! And that's exactly where the Alice Cooper group stepped into the breach. Audiences that had once scoffed at their show were now replaced by young kids who sensed that rock 'n' roll music needed a new set of agent provocateurs in order to keep vibrant.

Alice Cooper, along with the later glam explosion of Elton John, David Bowie and Marc Bolan were just the brash showmen that teenagers had been waiting for — the new aristocracy. Alice with his dark make-up and ripped tights took his place alongside Ziggy's screw down hairdo, Elton's ostrich feathers and Bolan's corkscrew curls as the abiding images of a time when over-the-top became de-rigeur. The glam fashion was to dress in outrageous satin outfits, eye shadow and thigh high platform boots. But somehow the sight of five tall, strapping American guys dolled-up like that, seemed all the more incongruous and imposing when set alongside the willowy femininity of the glam bands.

The dawning of the new decade had witnessed the Alice Cooper group's move to Warner Brothers. Teaming up with producer Bob Ezrin, they more than rose to the challenge of promotion to a major label by recording a brace of classic teenage anthems. "I'm Eighteen" and "School's Out" were direct appeals to young people the world over.

By now their singer, one Vincent Furnier, had fully adopted the alter ego of Alice Cooper. Here was a sexually ambiguous, violent persona you loved to hate — an evil, cynical and debauched character who drunk endless beer, courted danger and controversy and was killed nightly on stage — first in the electric chair, then hung, then guillotined. Alice always got his come-uppance. A cartoon character "bad guy".

Even in the heartland of middle America, where you would have expected five guys in make-up to go down like a lead balloon, the Alice Cooper group were incredibly popular. Maybe Lou Reed or Iggy Pop had cornered the market in hip credibility, holding sway with the rock journalists, but it was the Alice Cooper band that had the mass appeal factor down to a tee. They hit a nerve with typical American teenagers craving black humour and over the top melodrama. It was the sort of travelling rock 'n' roll theatre which had never been tried on such a scale before. It was always visually confrontational, sometimes camp, but rarely boring.

Of course the band had their detractors — many thought they had dragged rock into a state of almost self-parody. Pantomime dames with electric guitars. But to those who appreciated the shock horror and humour of it all — which included celebrity fans like Salvador Dali, George Burns and Liza Minnelli — it was gloriously over-the-top Americana.

Success and notoriety finally meant they were forever trying to live up to their image — not to mention a reckless, fast living and carefree lifestyle. In reality the band were never as outrageous as the publicity and hype often portrayed them. Even so, money was spent like it was going out of fashion, hotel rooms got trashed, private jets hired, the whole bit. If you caught the plane with Alice's name on it, it was best not to mind a bit of turbulence.

After a period of truly being at the peak of their profession — record breaking tours, number one albums and adoring hordes of fans — the band began to creak under the pressure. Worries started to surface that the show had moved too far in the direction of a showbizzy, vaudeville, top hat and tails act and away from basic rock 'n' roll. As a result, the personality of Alice the singer became increasingly detached from the rest of the group. By 1974 they couldn't keep up with the momentum of the monster they had created. The split, when it came, was an inevitable outcome of always trying to outdo themselves, not to mention the strain of constantly being on the road.

Michael Bruce experienced first hand the traumas of trying to keep the band on track, dealing with a public who increasingly associated the name of Alice Cooper with the lead singer alone. Of course the singer, one Vincent Furnier, still uses the name Alice Cooper, but that is another story. For many older fans, Alice needed his band as much as his band needed him. So far any long-lasting reunion has not been forthcoming, but the power of the music they made together remains a testament to a great band.

So Andy, now that you're my not-so-little brother, I don't think endless early exposure to the Alice Cooper group has scarred you for life psychologically — at least 25 years on I'm not aware that you have turned into an axe-wielding, serial killing maniac. But I suppose I ought to thank you, firstly for not being a normal little five year old and buying an Osmonds record. Secondly through you (and the Alice Cooper group) I got a kick up the arse at a time when I was in danger of getting lost in a maze of progressive virtuosos. I was reminded that rock n' roll was never supposed to be a serious academic exercise, it should be dangerous but also fun, it should shock your parents — and above all, it should be entertainment.

For me, Alice Cooper opened the way toward Roxy Music (the support act at that Wembley concert they tried to ban), David Bowie, Alex Harvey, Mott The Hoople and Thin Lizzy, and away from a cavalcade of pompous old tosh that I won't dignify with a mention. Suffice to say, much of punk rock took its inspiration from shock rock bands like The New York Dolls, The Stooges, and although a lot of them wouldn't admit it, even Alice Cooper. (Certainly, Johnny Rotten auditioned for his role as singer in the Sex Pistols by miming to an Alice Cooper record. Also Nick Cave's first band used to do Alice Cooper covers). Suffice to say, by the time punk came along I had already experienced make-up, ripped T-shirts, outrage and over-the-top live performances. And I was ready for more. *Killer* still sounds like a mighty fine record to me (OK, so I also went out and bought the CD). A bit rough around the edges by today's standards maybe, but still packed with great tunes.

Which brings us back to Michael Bruce, the man who came up with many of those tunes. His solid rhythm playing and keyboard embellishments always provided the backbone to the group's sound. Add to that Neal Smith's pounding beat, Dennis Dunaway's pumping bass, Glen Buxton's hard rock riffing, and of course, Alice's fine vocals and showmanship, then you had a true band sound. They were a real rock outfit that knew what they wanted to achieve. And what they did achieve was six gold albums and four platinum ones in the US alone. I guess there are not that many songwriters around that can make that claim! Now, with this fly-on-the-wall romp through his years with the group, fasten your seat belts, as Michael tells us how it all happened.

Dave Hallbery,
Editor, London.

The Early Years

I just lost it when I saw Elvis on the Ed Sullivan Show. I knew I had to do something in music but I wasn't quite sure what. My cousin played the guitar, so pretty soon when I was in high school in the early 60's, I got a guitar of my own. I had also picked up some piano because my mother had sung and played piano at USO shows at airforce bases in Arizona after the Second World War. Steve Allen also sung and played piano on these USO shows.

Then a few years went by and The Beatles happened and that's when I really found my calling. Like most of my generation, The Beatles were a great inspiration to me. As a result I got into the whole early British music scene — The Yardbirds, The Pretty Things, The Who etc. Back in the early sixties there was a club in Phoenix called The VIP which was a test club for a lot of European acts — groups like The Hollies, The Animals, The Yardbirds and Them all performed there. We saw all those groups which in turn became quite an influence on the early Alice Cooper group — you only have to listen to our first album *Pretties For You* to spot the influences. As well as digging the way these bands sounded, I was also impressed by the way those guys looked. That whole notion that we could be flashy dressers and have a greater visual impact than most of the other bands around came from the early days at the VIP club.

I first met Dennis Dunaway (b. 1948, Cottage Grove, Oregon) in 1963. He was the bass player in a band he had formed called The Spiders — a typical

Left: The "All American Boy", playing football at North High School.

Below: My first band The Duels, a rock n' roll combo available for school dances, private parties and fraternities.

Bottom: The Duels play a talent contest in Phoenix.

Photos: Michael Bruce collection

SCHOOL DANCES   PRIVATE PARTIES   FRATERNITIES

"THE DUELS"
Rock'N' Roll Combo

ROGER FEENOR
266-6730

MIKE BRUCE
266-5424

ONE OF FIVE BANDS — This group called "The Duels" was one of the five bands that entertained at the Nov. 1 CYO dance closing Catholic Youth Week in Phoenix. More than 1,000 teen-agers attended the event in the Phoenix Star Theatre.

sixties US garage band. At the time they were one of the biggest groups in Arizona. Dennis was really the leader of The Spiders. Back then he talked a lot more, he was a typical teenager. The Spiders singer was Vincent Furnier (Alice), a preacher's son who originally came from Detroit. Then there was Glen Buxton (from Akron, Ohio), John Speer and John Tatum. At the time I was in a band called The Trolls (formerly The Duels) and I would occasionally bump into them, usually during the "battle of the bands" shows. To me they looked like kids from *West Side Story* — I remember Dennis had a car with mag wheels — you know, "real cool man".

Dennis, Vince and Glen had all met whilst at Cortez High School. Dennis, John Speer and Vince were all on the track team together. Vince was a keen cross country runner, he broke his nose when he fell and cracked it on a curb after running the Phoenix marathon. Together with Glen, they were also on the school paper called *The Tipsheet*. Glen was the photographer, Vince the editor, and they covered anything to do with sport. "We all joined the paper because that's where all the neat girls were supposed to be," Dennis commented later.

Of course we all realised that a sure-fire way of attracting attention from the opposite sex was to be in a band. Dennis, Vince, Glen and John Speer had decided to form a proper group after doing a spoof spot at the Cortez talent show representing the Lettermen's Club. They had showed up in Beatle wigs and were naturally impressed by the way they received screaming adulation from the girls, even though they weren't actually in a band as such. Originally called The Earwigs, they teamed up with John Tatum and changed their name to The Spiders.

One day I got a call that The Spiders needed a guitarist as Tatum had left their band. They were aware of me because I had started a band called The Wildflowers, and we had gone as far a recording a 7" single called "On A Day Like Today" backed with "A Man Like Myself". The record got a bit of local airplay. So I went over and auditioned for The Spiders. They never actually told me I was in the band, but I had a van with plenty of room to carry gear around. I think they wanted the van more than me. But all in all I guess I was in the right place at the right time.

At that time The Spiders were playing mainly Rolling Stones' songs, so much so that before joining them I used to call them the Rolling Clones. They were good at mimicking styles, Alice had the harmonica solo from "I'm

Left: Happy Christmas from The Trolls, 1966.
Above: The Trolls - Bill Parins, Roger Fleenor, Mike Millar and myself.
Below: Bill Parins, myself, Roger Fleenor and Mike Millar.
Photos: Michael Bruce collection

21

A Man" down note-for-note. For a while, I didn't want them to know I was recording music on the side, so I changed my name to Bruce Michael for the second Wildflowers 7" record called "More Than Me" backed with "Moving Along With The Sun". I kept this pseudonym thing going for a while.

The Wildflowers played original material, so one day I turned round to the rest of The Spiders and said, "Hey, let's start writing our own songs, instead of mainly doing cover versions." Dennis thought that was cool — he said he had some songs. So the first couple of songs we wrote together were "Don't Blow Your Mind" and "Pricetag". Later we wrote "Wonder Who's Loving Her Now" and "Lay Down And Die Goodbye" (the original version).

Back then, Dennis was kind of the leader of the band. I remember when I first joined he told me, "You have to learn to move around on stage". Even early on he was quite the showman and a big asset to the way the band developed. He was always pushing for us to be more esoteric and underground rather than commercial and accessible. In any event, we started to write a lot of tunes together.

Then one day we were rehearsing over at Glen's house. John Speer, our drummer, had a real attitude and a temper — a real short fuse. So anyway, John said something that annoyed Dennis — to this day I don't know what he said — but Dennis threw his bass down and dived over the drums on John, and just went at it right there in the Buxton's house. Normally, Dennis was so quiet. I guess he was tired of John's shit. Anyway, after their fight John was real quiet most of the time.

Being from Arizona, the band developed a tough hide by playing a lot of gigs in and around Phoenix. As well as playing at the VIP on the weekend we were also getting other gigs in the area, even doing a bit of local TV. If we had been from San Francisco or LA, it would have been easier for us. But playing in a long-haired, psychedelic band that dressed all flashy made us an easy target in Arizona. So, very early on we learned how to deal with a hostile reaction, not to mention a considerable amount of violence.

Growing up in Arizona in the sixties, essentially there were two opposing gangs of kids — the redneck cowboys and the Indians from the reservation. It goes without saying that the cowboy rednecks were prejudiced against the Indians out there. So they used to run out to the reservation, get drunk and start fights. So when us long hairs came along, both the rednecks and the Indians turned on us. We were caught in the middle.

Guns were just part of life out in Arizona. Anyone could carry a hand gun, no permit was necessary. Glen and Neal used to go out into the desert for shooting practice. Neal Smith, who was then the drummer in a band called The Holy Grail, had started to hang out with us and had bought a Thompson machine gun. Glen had some Derringers. Neal also had swords as far as I can remember.

One time we played this show in Chandler, Arizona and this guy came right up to us in the middle of our show and flashed a switchblade at us. It wasn't that unusual for us to get chased out of town. We'd have beer bottles thrown at us, you name it. At the end of another show we had to stay inside the National Guard armoury because the cowboys and the Indians had lined up outside ready to beat the hell out of us. It was a bit like something out of a Western.

But we grew up in a violent era, Vietnam was happening. I suppose it was a good grounding for the group, we were used to seeing fights. Later on, we wanted to throw that violence back in people's faces. On stage, for theatrical reasons, we didn't so much want to portray that we were violent but that the world is a violent place by making a mockery of it.

In any event, some time in the spring of 1968 we decided that the band would stand a better chance of receiving a reaction and getting a record deal if we moved to LA. We reckoned, at the very least, that we could go back to play in Phoenix and say, "Just back from LA", as a way of getting more money. And it worked. We all moved into this real neat house in the Hollywood Hills that was owned by John Phillip Law who had played the angel in the film *Barbarella*. Neal and I shared a room. Alice lived in the basement and Glen lived off the kitchen. The house was like a scaled-down mansion, it had a swimming pool out the back. A lot of the Beatles-influenced songs that were on the first two albums were written there. It was a real communal set-up. We kind of liked the communal thing, I think we were probably one of the last real communal bands.

Neal and I were probably the closest, even though he was still officially to join the band. We all knew Neal from back in the Phoenix days, as we'd often played gigs with his band The Holy Grail. I remember one time when we did a gig with them at this airforce base in Tucson, Arizona. Neal and this drummer friend of mine, Mike, found this amplifier — I guess one of the other bands playing the gig had left it behind. "Hey you can hide it in my car", I foolishly volunteered.

KFIF SALUTES
THE SPIDERS

It's amazing to keep tabulation of the number of bands that have come into existence during the past couple of years. Tucson alone can claim a list to make your head spin. Then there are out of town bands -- bands from every corner of Arizona. For any band to establish a statewide reputation of being great is no easy task. But 5 guys from Phoenix have done just that. And they call themselves the Spiders. No need to tell you about the "sound" the Spiders put out. Just about everyone in Tucson has heard them wail. It's enough to lift you 10 feet off the ground. Their recent recording of "Don't Blow Your Mind" was one of the strongest sounds of 1966 and we understand the Spider's newest release will be available soon.

The Spiders were organized about 3 years ago and their aim is to stay together, develop their own sound, and write songs in their own style. They've accomplished a great part of this already. Their material is presented to enthusiastic audiences everywhere with all the flair and drive of the professionals they are.

KFIF tips its BOSS hat to one of the top groups in the state -- THE SPIDERS. With so much talent brought together in one group we know they'll remain high on the list of favorites for a long, long time to come.

Photos:
Henry Harvey
Phoenix

MIKE BRUCE   **JOHN SPEER**   **VINCE FURNIER
                                                & GLEN BUXTON**   **DENNIS DUNAWAY**

Opposite left: Tucson American, Jan 25th 1967. An early Spiders gig.

Other photos: The Spiders line-up, Vincent Furnier, Dennis Dunaway, John Speer, Glen Buxton and myself.

So, later the guy who owned the amp came back looking all over for it. At that time I owned a Corvair which was a really small car but had a large trunk in the front, so the amp fit perfectly. Well, he looked everywhere for it, but didn't ask me to open the trunk. So, we got away with it. When we got back to Phoenix I asked them, "What are you going to do with the amp?" And they said, "probably sell it". So I said, "Well, tell you what, I'll trade you my Fender amp and sell that instead because its not hot". They said, "OK".

Then I fixed it up, put new knobs and a solid cover back on it, thinking that would be enough to fool anyone who might suspect. Well the next time the band played in Tucson, the police walked up on stage, escorted me off and promptly arrested me. Obviously, my parents were real upset and had to pay $500, which was a lot of money back then, to get me out of trouble. So I had to get a job as a busboy at a restaurant to pay them back. I remember being furious because it meant missing the original season of *Star Trek*!

What the band all had in common was a background in the arts. Vince (Alice), Dennis, Glen and Neal were all arts majors. Many of the later theatrics came from this grounding, the general feeling emerged that we should try and employ artistic and theatrical ideas and translate these into a rock band. Just to do something that nobody had done before. The basic idea was to have people come to the shows and not forget the band — we were prepared to do whatever it took to make that happen.

Vince and I very rarely did things together other than band stuff. For the most part we didn't really have a lot in common. He didn't play any sports other than running, I was into football and tennis. Also he didn't play an instrument. I guess Vince considered himself a bit of an intellectual. His father was a priest and they came from an upper middle class neighbourhood in Arizona — a real nice house.

By the time we moved to Hollywood, we had changed our name from The Spiders to The Nazz. The name was taken from the comic Lord Buckley's nickname for Jesus the Nazarene. Almost as soon as we'd done that Todd Rundgren came out with a record by his group called The Nazz. So instantly we needed a new name.

The Alice Cooper name came about when Vince sat down one night with our road manager Dick Phillips, his sister Bonnie Phillips and their mother who was supposed to be a medium. They were playing the Ouija board and Vince asked it who he had been in a past life. The board spelled out the name

Alice Cooper. It was only later that Sherry Cottle from the Cheetah Club embellished this by adding the bit about Alice Cooper supposedly being the name of a 16th century English witch. That sounded like good publicity to us so we ran with it.

But at the time we were looking at all these different names, and at first we thought the name sounded too strange and we decided against it. Then one night we all got together and went over to the road manager's house for a meeting. Oddly enough, everybody had quite dramatically changed their minds and it was agreed that we would become the Alice Cooper group.

Talking of seances, reminds me of the time Jim Morrison came to our house in the Los Angeles hills on Halloween night. We were having this big seance. David Crosby was there and so was Arthur Lee of Love. I remember we were all holding hands in a big circle. I was holding Jim's hand and he turned to me and said, "Do you guys do this stuff all the time?" And I said, "No, actually this is the first time". I think because of our freaky appearance and the way we had arrived at our name, everyone assumed we were doing that sort of thing constantly. But Jim Morrison was a really nice guy. We hung out with Robbie Krieger too. Janis Joplin used to be around as well. We did some gigs with her at the Cheetah Club in LA. She was really loose in those early days.

It was real nice back then. The music community was still quite small and sooner or later you pretty much met most people. Eventually everyone would end up at the Landmark Hotel when they came out to Los Angeles — it was like the place to be. I remember Jimi Hendrix was real laid back, very likeable. We first met him out in Tucson, Arizona. Les Braiden, who worked with Pink Floyd, Cream, and also us, got us backstage to some of Hendrix's shows. We hung out with him a bit, but I think few people really got to know Jimi that well because he was so busy with touring etc.

One time we were all in a hotel room with Jimi, and someone was passing around the acid. Jimi was sitting on the bed with this big old kilo of marijuana and he would put a dime in the magic fingers and say things like, "Come on, get on my rocket ship", Jimi was like "Wow" — super stoned out of his fucking mind. He was out there big time. He told me he really liked Arizona. Another time we went to this party with Hendrix and this hypnotist called Doctor Donte was there. He hypnotized a bunch of people and told them to act out being their favourite musician — so some of those in a trance became Hendrix and would mimic all his moves etc. I remember Jimi being particu-

larly amused by this. He sat there and laughed his ass off.

Of course, being big Pink Floyd fans we were all thrilled when Syd Barrett came to Los Angeles. He was the first real space-case I ever met — he was completely out there. He wouldn't look at you so much as look through you — he was somewhere else. He would be playing on stage and suddenly drift off, stop playing. He would just stand there with his guitar right in the middle of a song and the other guys would just keep playing. I guess this must have happened a lot because it didn't seem to phase them at all. He was a real trip to watch. He was definitely the first cosmic cowboy I ever ran across.

We had asked Sherry Cottle from the Cheetah Club to bring the Pink Floyd to Los Angeles because they were playing at the other Cheetah Clubs. As we were big fans of theirs, Sherry made sure that the whole of Pink Floyd came to see us play at some club in LA. Alice really wanted to impress them because we all thought *Piper At The Gates Of Dawn* was amazing, so he ate some marijuana brownies. He was standing on stage and suddenly just passed out. He fell face forward on the ground and everyone thought, "Wow, that's neat", believing it to be part of the show.

This was the final straw for John Speer. He got really mad about Alice eating the pot brownies. So, the next day he loaded his car and went back to Phoenix. As Neal was already staying with us at the house in Hollywood, he just started playing with us right away. Once Neal joined, the music took a radical change of direction because Neal was a very different type of drummer. At six foot three, he was a walking billboard. He was outrageous even then — with his really long hair he had exactly the right look for the stage show we were developing. Neal's drum style was like night and day compared with John because he didn't have that heavy foot feel. He had been influenced by the big band drummers of the fifties, like Sandy Nelson and Gene Krupa. Like the rest of us, he was a big Beatles and Stones fan, but the rock drummers he looked up to most were people like Ginger Baker, Keith Moon and Mitch Mitchell. He was also very creative — he played a bit of guitar and piano. With his flailing arms, he soon amassed an alarmingly large kit which he would pound with a kind of tribal ferocity.

It was once Neal had joined that we really started to develop the psychedelic angle of the band. We liked the way Pink Floyd played around with sound in those early days. Also, Neal was into Stockhausen and that European avant-garde kind of music. It was this that influenced us to try and play music that used the basic two guitars, bass, drums and singer format, but in a way that sounded like nobody had ever heard before. I remember we would also do a lot of fooling around, like driving out into the desert to these picnic areas and taking peyote. One particular night we were watching the stars come up and we were all so stoned we thought we saw a flying saucer. On closer inspection, this actually turned out to be the planet Venus!

Talking of stars, we also opened for Led Zeppelin on their first US tour when they played the Whisky-A-Go-Go in Hollywood. It was their first gig in the United States. What happened was they played this first week with us and then cancelled the rest of the shows because they all came down with the Hong Kong flu. Well, we were really pissed off and had to finish the rest of the shows with Buddy Miles headlining.

Pretties For You

Once we had changed our name to the Alice Cooper group, Dennis slowly started to withdraw from being the leader of the group. I think one of the reasons for this was that at that time he was involved with this girl Paula Heater and this kinda put the brakes on him. She told him that she was pregnant so Dennis had to wrestle with the decision of whether to stay in Hollywood with the band or quit and go back to Phoenix to take care of her. She didn't want to come out to Los Angeles as she was young and her parents probably wouldn't have let her go anyway. He decided to stay with the band — which was lucky for us, particularly as Dennis was well liked, everyone had a lot of respect for him. He was also a very underrated bassist. He had his own very unique style. A lot of stuff that bands are doing now, that Rotosound bass, sounds like Dennis. Even early on he played with a sort of Indian raga style.

Life in the early days revolved around going into the city to do this or that, trying to get gigs, trying to get laid, trying to eat. It was a meagre existence. It was around that time that the whole band was involved in a bad road accident. One day we were on our way back from Phoenix and somebody had cut us off on the freeway and our truck flipped end-over-end three times. It rolled upside down and smashed into the road bank and everything flew out. Luckily, we had loaded the gear into the van and then put a carpet on top so we could all ride in the back. Basically, it was this carpet which saved us from getting crushed to death. Amazingly none of us was badly hurt.

The truck didn't fare so well and was a complete write off. For a while it was difficult to get to gigs and we had to rely on our girlfriends to come over with their vehicles to drive us around. So sometimes we'd be late or some of our gear wouldn't show up at all. Later on, the accident was used as a promotional device. We dreamed up the notion that it would make for good press if we said we all had died in the accident and been reborn as the Alice Cooper group.

At this point, it is important to remember that the name Alice Cooper was the collective name of the group way before Vince actually became the character Alice Cooper. Obviously, the very name by its nature did cause quite a lot of interest. It was a good talking point. I guess five guys calling themselves Alice Cooper wasn't exactly what a lot people were expecting at the time. In fact, it was not uncommon for those who knew nothing about the group to expect some blonde long haired folk songstress and her backing band to turn up. Inevitably people would ask, "So, where's this girl Alice?"

It was only later, when it became clear that Vince was a natural mouthpiece for the band, that he actually became Alice. But it was a joint decision. We all sat down and decided, "Why couldn't Vince become Alice" — thus we created a monster.

It was natural that Vince became the spokesman for a band called Alice Cooper. Not only was he the singer, but he had a good line in witty remarks. Originally we were having some problems when we'd go to do a radio interview. Five different guys all talking at the same time and trying to answer questions just didn't work very well. Somehow playing the character of Alice, Vince could get away with more outrageous comments than he could have merely as the band's singer. As the Alice character took over, the whole philosophy of the band shifted farther and farther away from some of the more obscure and avant-garde ideas that Dennis, in particular, had envisioned for the group. Dennis was originally "Mr. Avant Garde", he was into art and painting. He really liked to think up obscure ideas for the band.

Creating the persona of Alice seemed to do the trick when it came to getting ourselves noticed. Increasingly Vince began to treat the name Alice Cooper like it was an alter ego which he would refer to in the third person, "Alice does this, Alice thinks this", and so on. Just like an actor entering into his role, he would take to the stage, not as Vince Furnier, preacher's son and rock 'n' roll singer, but as Alice Cooper the supposedly reincarnated sixteenth century English witch. I think it gave him the chance to be outrageous. Just as Vince had acquired a new personality as Alice, so the rest of us were also given mythological, almost medieval, personalities. An early feature on the band gave us each these rather quaint descriptions:

"Glen Buxton, lead guitarist, is described by Alice as a 'brooding figure of the past, a black knight once feared by many... come to tell of centuries of hate and a world of fear'."

"Dennis Dunaway, bass guitarist, is an 'artist of the courts painting the picture of history, knowing the colours of tomorrow'."

"Michael Bruce, rhythm guitarist, is a 'poet of the streets, writing songs of centuries, a figure in the fields of tomorrow'. "

Neal Smith, drummer, is a warrior king, born of power, bred in the stronghold of the gods. He is here now, leading Alice toward the future of yesterday'."

I think Sherry Cottle from the Cheetah Club in LA where we played quite regularly, dreamt up these descriptions. Our reputation for being a bit "weird" was enhanced by the fact that we would walk around in the same clothes that we wore on stage. It was quite natural to us to dress flamboyantly, but I think some people thought we were a bunch of transvestites or something, especially since we were in a band called Alice Cooper. A woman's name, guys with super long hair and female looking clothes, I guess people were always going to jump to the wrong conclusions. But we were never a jeans and T-shirts type band.

Cindy Smith (Neal Smith's sister) had a clothing boutique that she was running with a girl named Linda Lease. Having a seamstress connected with the band was a definite advantage as she would make some of the clothes we would wear. We also bought a lot of the early clothes at flea markets. Marshal Brevits had a place called the Psychedelic Supermarket which was a space where he rented out stalls to little crafts and candle makers, tie-dye shirt vendors, hippie shops. We used to rehearse there at night. I remember one gig I wore these transparent plastic pants Cindy Smith had made for me, which I was kind of embarrassed to wear because you could see everything! However, by the time I got on stage they had fogged up from sweating. Our idea was to hit the audience on a lot of different levels, not only lyrically and musically, but also visually. I think it captured people's imaginations.

At the time we were doing all the usual things like walking up and down Sunset Strip, shopping our tape around. We got an audition for the original Sound label (Music Machines label) so we played "Talk Talk" and a bunch of other songs and they were really impressed. But then they said, "The only trouble is we don't like that Vince guy. We will sign you right now if you get rid of him". Well, that really pissed us off and we said, "No man, we're a band." It was a good thing we didn't follow their advice or there never would have been an Alice Cooper group.

One day these two fast talking guys, Joe Greenberg and Shep Gordon, came in Cindy's boutique, talking about how they had just come out to LA from Buffalo Business College and were now managing bands including the Left Banke. Cindy told them, "Oh, my brother's in a band". So they came out to Topanga Canyon in this old fucked up, beat up Cadillac to see us. Well they liked the band, and said they would like to manage us.

By then we were already talking to Frank Zappa about a record deal. Because of our long hair and strange clothes some people were associating us with the freak scene in LA which was based around Frank Zappa and the Mothers Of Invention. Zappa had set up a record label called Straight, whose policy was to sign bands and artists who were anything but straight ahead rock. I guess Zappa saw his label not only as a commercial exercise and a way of sticking two fingers up at his previous record label, but also as an opportunity to release records by the most unlikely and freaky people that amused him. I guess he considered we fitted the bill.

We had originally heard about the Straight auditions when we were doing this gig with Blue Cheer and the Nitty Gritty Dirt Band. One of the guys in the NGDB told us about Frank's label and said, "You guys are crazy enough to be on Zappa's label." But it wasn't until we played the Lenny Bruce festival in Santa Monica that we actually met Zappa himself. This was an annual event called the Lenny Brucemas which was held at the Cheetah Club in Venice, CA. It was the first time Zappa heard us play live.

Well, we managed to clear the hall of 3,000 people after just two numbers. Apparently the only people remaining at the end of the set were Frank Zappa, Shep Gordon and several members of the GTO's. I suppose our ability to outrage and upset people appealed to Zappa, who himself was not unused to ruffling the odd feather of authority.

In any event, we auditioned for Frank Zappa at his log cabin house in Laurel Canyon. Frank told us to come over and audition at 6:30. Well for some reason we thought he meant 6:30 in the morning. So we got there that early, set up our equipment, and began playing in his basement.

Then Frank comes downstairs looking like he just woke up, with a cup of coffee in his hand and says, "What the fuck is going on here? I meant 6:30 at night."

"Well we're here now, we might as well continue", we said. So, a bleary-eyed Zappa listened to us audition. We played "10 Minutes Before The Worm", "BB On Mars", and "Lay Down and Die Goodbye" and Zappa promptly said, "You got the deal". We had no hesitation in taking it. Frank said, "Come around tomorrow night and my manager Herb Cohen will be here to sign you up".

So, when we told everyone the good news, Joe Greenberg and Shep Gordon said to us, "Let us represent you. We'll tell them that we manage you and that way we'll get a better deal for you."

So we did. That next night Joe and Shep went over to meet with Herb Cohen and told him that they were the managers of the Alice Cooper group. We signed with Straight Records and Shep and Joe acted as our managers. I think Frank and Herb were a bit upset about this — in effect it meant they couldn't totally control us. I really feel it was one reason we weren't buried alive by them. For the most part, all the other bands on the Straight label never really did anything. Secretly I think the other acts were mainly tax write-offs.

Anyway, the net result was that at least we had a record deal, even if I was actually too young to legally sign the record contract. In the end my parents had to sign the deal for me. It was just before my 21st birthday.

After getting the deal we did a show with the Mothers, Captain Beefheart, Easy Chair, GTOs, and Wildman Fisher at the Shrine Auditorium in LA in 1969. Kim Fowley also got up and did a few numbers. It was quite a crazy bill when you come to think about it, everything from a blues act to Wildman Fisher. The Mothers were very friendly toward us, so this led to us hanging out and playing gigs together with them all around the southern Californian area. I'm sure a lot people assumed that we got our weirdness from The Mothers, but that really wasn't the case. We were well into weirdness back in Arizona. We were doing all that well before we met Zappa and the Mothers.

4

5 | Attorney for Petitioner

6

7

8 | SUPERIOR COURT OF THE STATE OF CALIFORNIA

9 | FOR THE COUNTY OF LOS ANGELES

10

11 | BIZARRE RECORDS INC.)

12 | Petitioner,)   NO.

13 | and   ) STIPULATION WAIVING NOTICE OF TIME AND
    |) PLACE OF HEARING OF PETITION FOR APPROVAL
14 | MICHAEL BRUCE   ) OF A MINOR'S CONTRACT

15 | Minor.   )

16 | _____)

17 | IT IS HEREBY STIPULATED AND AGREED between the above-named petitioner,

18 | the above-named minor and the parents of the minor that the petition in the above-

19 | entitled matter for approval of the minor's contract under Section 36 of the Califor-

20 | nia Civil Code may be heard in the courtroom of Department 1 of the Superior Court

21 | of the County of Los Angeles or in any department of said Court to which it is

22 | assigned at any time after this date, without any other or further notice, such

23 | notice being expressly waived.

24 | Dated:

25

26 | _____
    | Herbert L. Cohen

27

28 | _____
    | Minor

29

30 | _____
    | Parent

31

32 | _____
    | Parent

STATE OF ARIZONA
COUNTY OF MARICOPA
This instrument was acknowledged before me this 16th day of September 1968
By Alvin Bruce and Ruth Bruce.

_____
Notary

My Commission Expires June 25, 1972

Above: The contract with Bizarre which required my parents' signatures, as I was still classified a minor by law.

Frank Zappa was very talented and creative, although to me kind of odd. I remember when we were recording our first album *Pretties For You*, the band were smoking a joint in the studio bathroom. Well, Zappa smelled it and knocked on the door and told us to get out and go into the alley and smoke it because he didn't want to get in trouble with the studio owners. So, now there's a bunch of long hairs standing out in the alley where we might get busted. Being Los Angeles in the late 60's it wasn't the smartest thing to do — this was right after the Watts riots, things were pretty crazy then.

One night we met at Frank's house on Mulholland Drive to discuss ideas for our first LP. Zappa wanted us to package the album in a cookie tin and change the name of the band to the Alice Cookies group. There would be twelve little hip pocket records (small acetates about the size of a CD) and you had a little player that played these things — anyway we would have been called the Alice Cookies Group and the records would come in a cookie tin! Well, we all thought that this was very cute but hardly the most commercial idea we'd come across. Essentially, we didn't think we'd sell a bucket load of albums that way. So we stuck with the name Alice Cooper. Then Zappa had the idea of putting the album out in tuna fish cans, but that didn't happen either.

In the end Frank did get us to put the painting by Ed Beardsley on the front cover of Pretties For You. For the back cover we had Ed Cariff take a lot of the photos of the band at this art exhibition, so that's why there are all those car parts in the background.

Originally the record was supposed to have been produced by Frank himself, but he mysteriously became ill. Maybe he was just sick of us! I think by the late sixties he was considerably over stretching himself with various projects as well as touring extensively. It was this that had prompted him to disband the original Mothers Of Invention, as well as giving up on producing our album. Maybe, it was also becoming obvious to him that he couldn't mould us in the direction that Straight wanted.

In the end, our first album was mainly produced by Ian Underwood of the Mothers Of Invention, who for some reason did not get a credit on the record. Most of the tracks we recorded live with very little overdubbing. Maybe we overdubbed a few of the vocals. Then after the album was finished, Herbie (Herb Cohen) didn't like the mix on a couple of songs. So he came in to the studio with us one night to remix them. He was so bored he fell asleep on the couch. He finally turned the project back over to Ian who finished it. The album was recorded on a 16-track recorder at Whitney Studios in Burbank, where they had a huge pipe organ on which I recorded the organ part to the "Titanic Overture".

I am not sure the album really turned out to Zappa's satisfaction. Unlike the other acts on Straight, we clearly had our own ideas. I think it was becoming apparent to him that we weren't quite the act that he had expected when he signed us. "Well maybe I don't know your music after all, maybe I should have listened to it some more," was his comment. I remember Alice later complaining to *Rolling Stone* that Zappa had acted a bit like a dictator, "Frank didn't take us seriously. He thought of us as freaks like the GTO's and we aren't".

When it came to the songwriting on *Pretties For You*, I basically started the germs of most of those songs, then everybody added their two-cents worth. At that time the deal was if you had a song, anyone in the band could add to it musically — truly a band scenario. In a way it was neat because you'd get a lot of ideas, but from a songwriter's standpoint it really sucked. With five people all chipping in ideas, it was like having five chefs trying to cook a bowl of soup — all this stuff just coming out of left field.

"BB On Mars" was written with the concept of the size of an actual BB (an air rifle) On Mars — how really small that was.

"Levity Ball" was recorded live at the Cheetah Club on a two track Telefunken recorder. The main inspiration for the song came from a classic horror movie called *Carnival Of Souls*. It was filmed out in Great Salt Lake and featured all these dead zombies walking around as if they had too much starch in their clothes. We tried to imagine what would we have produced musically if we had done the soundtrack to this movie. The lyrics were about a birthday party — candles on the cake — but it's really about getting high and drugs.

While we were writing "Living" I remember walking around with Alice on the beach talking about lyrics. We were walking together and it's the only time I can really remember being that close to him. From then on we got farther and farther apart. Certainly at the time we wrote "Living" the band was totally of one mind. We were all contributing material, "Apple Bush" for instance was a song that Neal had written. I think it was about the apple in the Garden of Eden — heavy stuff!

Pretties For You was released at the end of 1969, reaching No 193 in the US charts. The reviews picked up on the fact that we were a band hooked

Above: The bathroom photo session at LAX in California. Could this be the
early makings of the classic "Flush The Fashion"?
Opposite top: The band in dark and mysterious guise
Opposite bottom: Alice and myself with facial hair much in vogue

41

on the Beatles and Stones but with a nascent interest in the camp and glitzy side of showbiz. It's true we had plundered bits and pieces of Burt Bacharach, *West Side Story* and James Bond movie themes for ideas. I remember Alice commenting some years later that, "We swiped about eleven bits from the *Goldfinger* soundtrack on the first album, just redid them on guitar. Nobody noticed!" In fact, we borrowed several bits, learned them backwards, and then played them for the record.

We played a few shows around Los Angeles to promote the *Pretties For You* album but at that time the competition was The Doors, Three Dog Night, Buffalo Springfield, it was rough for us in that sort of illustrious company. I remember when Frank had us play at the Whiskey-A-Go-Go for these Warner Bros record executives. We opened with this song "Come With Us Now" (a demo version of which was only recorded recently on Ant-Bee's latest CD single "Child Of The Moon" — Divine records, UK). It was sort of a Burt Bacharach style song — definitely not an Alice Cooper type song per se. It was a very light, mellow beginning to the show, it kind of lulled the audience into a false sense of security. Then Bam! and we'd go into "10 Minutes Before The Worm". Even then, the whole notion of contrast, the light and dark of a show, was something we were very interested in.

It was within this context that we started to concentrate on making the whole show as theatrical as possible. At first it was very simple ideas like Alice singing through a screen door during "Nobody Likes Me". From this we moved on to less workable ideas like the so-called "fire machine". In fact, I think we only used this once. Essentially, it was nothing more than a rectangular box the size of a phone booth with plastic streamers (like you see on car lots) hanging from it. We then set the streamers on fire. The problem was that the melting plastic dripped all over the stage and promptly set it ablaze too. Hence the arrival of the fire marshals who came up on stage and forced us to stop playing. We weren't sure whether they were complaining about the fire hazard, or the fact that it was in bad taste and bad theatre!

We liked the idea of experimenting with anything we thought would "blow people's minds". Our whole notion of a stage show seemed to be really disconnected with what was going on at the time in music. We felt we were much more in the showbiz tradition than those rock 'n' roll bands that put all the emphasis on the "music" and never really bothered to put on much of a show.

We realised early on that we needed something to set us apart. The early stage antics certainly did that, but they also bought us time to improve musically.

Admittedly, some of our antics were less successful than others. At one concert, we decided to stage a stunt based around the rumours which abounded about the cover to The Beatles' *Abbey Road* record. People were speculating that Paul McCartney had actually died because he was wearing no shoes on the album's cover shot of the four Beatles crossing the road in front of Abbey Road studios. So, for this particular show we all dressed in white, except for Dennis who came on dressed in black and wearing no shoes. We then ripped straight into a version of "Lay Down and Die Goodbye". I don't know how many of the audience got the joke, but we laughed all the way to the unemployment line.

Despite the occasional setback, our reputation — perhaps notoriety is a better word — was beginning to spread. We were actually becoming quite popular, not always for the right reasons. For a while, booing us off stage actually became quite the popular thing to do. But we had become hardened to it. When people shouted out things like, "You suck!", Alice would just retort, "Yes I do". Another joke that went around at the time was for people to say that they had only bought tickets for the show so that they could tell their friends that they had walked out on the Alice Cooper group! I guess that was fame of sorts.

One of the first signs that the tide was beginning to turn was when we played one our biggest shows yet. I remember it clearly because we were supporting Three Dog Night and the Buffalo Springfield in Orange County, California and it was one of the the first times we didn't get booed off stage! We actually went down well! Another time, we opened for The Doors at the Cheetah Club and we received a standing ovation. The Doors' manager freaked, he wouldn't let us go on for an encore. We must have scared him big time.

Alice in particular, had now developed a tough exterior which made us almost immune to insults and heckles. I think audiences turned from plain hating us, to us becoming the band they loved to hate. Vince in his new guise as Alice got used to encouraging derision, or berating and goading an audience into hating him, but in a playful kind of way. Both Frank Zappa and Jim Morrison had been known to tease and abuse an audience, but Alice would take it one stage further. I remember Lester Bangs reporting that he was impressed by an incident that happened when we played the Cincinnati

Pop Festival. After Alice had been pelted with a pie, rather than recoiling in horror, he made the most of the incident by smearing the pie all over his body. Bangs, although then not particularly a fan of ours, obviously considered it was a good way of silencing the critics.

In New York, Shep had run into Frank Perry, a director who was casting for the movie *Diary Of A Mad Housewife*. The film featured Richard Benjamin, Frank Langela, and Carrie Snodgrass (who later married Neil Young). I met Neil Young some years later at the Record Plant in Los Angeles and I told him about how I had met his ex-wife during the filming. He thought that it was a funny story. Anyway, they needed a band for the movie's party scene. So we were sent the sheet music to a song which Mars Bonfire had written especially for the movie which we then proceeded to learn. Bonfire had written "Born To Be Wild", but I don't think the particular tune we were given was one of his better songs. However, to spice up our performance in the movie we decided to use the feathers trick. This was another of our theatrical escapades where Alice would break open a down-feathered pillow on stage. We would then use CO_2 to blow feathers all over the place. The consequence was usually that a dense fog of feathers would cover the front few rows of the audience.

More famously, we were also featured in the movie of the Toronto Pop Festival which was organised by John Lennon and Yoko Ono in 1969. A sort rock 'n' roll revival show, the festival was an attempt to mix contemporary rock acts like the Plastic-Ono band, The Doors and ourselves with performances by traditional old rock 'n' rollers like Chuck Berry, Jerry Lee Lewis and Gene Vincent. I remember we were the backing band for Gene Vincent's set. I think Gene Vincent's appearance at the Festival had been pretty much arranged by Jim Morrison — the two of them had become drinking partners. Initially, The Doors were supposed to be backing him but due to scheduling problems we filled in instead.

I briefly met John and Yoko, but I was really too scared to talk to them. They were sitting backstage alone with this "presence" that seemed to surround them. I gingerly walked up to them and shook their hands. I did the usual star-struck number and mumbled what big a fan I was and then left. I really didn't want to bother them. Now I wish I'd have stayed and talked for a bit longer. Their set became the *Live Peace In Toronto* album. There have been several different releases of our performance ("Ladies Man", "Nobody Likes Me", etc, cd's) which we've never been paid for, incidentally. Also, Pennybaker shot a promo film of the whole event which featured a clip of our set, notably the incident when Alice threw a chicken into the audience.

The infamous chicken incident came about this way. Basically we'd had to ditch the feathers trick because both the club owners and the other bands we played with hated it — there would end up being feathers everywhere. I remember one time going back to play in this club that we had visited two or three months previously and there were still feathers floating around. So at Toronto we decided, rather than feathers, why not use the real thing? Why not throw chickens out. It was a camp inside joke. Evidently Alice, being a city boy, didn't know that the chickens couldn't fly. I mean I don't know if he was that naive or not, but when was the last time you saw a chicken fly by your window? But of course once the chickens had landed so to speak, we didn't have anything to do with whatever happened to them in the audience.

It has been said that the audience proceeded to tear the chickens to pieces. Alice later embellished this story by claiming that the front rows were reserved for those in wheelchairs and it was they who had been responsible for demise of the poor animals. In any event, the whole incident sparked off all sorts of rumours that spread like wildfire that we did extreme things to animals on stage, like dismembering chickens. Like many rumours, it soon became like a game of Chinese whispers — now the pillow of feathers had in fact been a sack of worms that got suspended and then unleashed over the audience! Clearly, we were getting the reputation as the bad boys of rock. Our love of shock theatrics was obviously gaining us a notoriety that was hardly in keeping with the so-called flower power generation.

In fact, one of my few memories of the original hippies was when we visited Dennis' grandparents in Eugene, Oregon. We had this big meal with vegetables and carrot juice and after the meal was over his grandfather said, "Hey, do you want to go over to the hippies' house?" We said, "Yeah, who's that?" He said, "Ken Kesey". So we got on the back of the flatbed truck and rode over there. Unfortunately, Ken Kesey (Merry Prankster and author of *One Flew Over The Cuckoo's Nest*) wasn't there, but the Merry Pranksters were busy painting their bus and some guy had an amplifier and mike and was narrating what was going on. So we hung out there for the day. They were getting ready for Woodstock. I suppose we should have just got on the bus and gone with them, but somehow I don't feel we were part of that Woodstock generation scene.

Alice later summed it up by saying that, "We were the ones who drove the stake through the heart of the peace and love generation". Certainly we were becoming further divorced from the hippie bands who we quite often shared bills with. I think many of the West Coast space jam bands hated our theatrics. I remember one occasion when we were scheduled to play with the Warner Bros acts touring as the Medicine Ball Caravan. When we reached Washington, Owsley's people who were controlling the PA refused to let us play. To us this seemed like a piece of gross hypocrisy. Suddenly these so called liberated individuals — Owsley was the guy who almost single-handedly created the San Francisco Acid Tests where they distributed LSD — were coming on all dictatorial. In the end a strange alliance of the Washington police, who escorted us on stage, and the Jefferson Airplane, who lent us their equipment, meant we could play our set.

In truth, I think our music was more inclined towards the seventies and a new generation of kids who were becoming tired of the hippie philosophy and the long extended blues jams that accompanied it. I guess with our flashy clothes, stage theatrics and macabre sense of humour, we were beginning to attract a new, largely teenage audience. In an attempt to reflect the violence that we saw going on around us, Alice and Neal had even developed a routine on stage where they got into a cat fight. Kids seemed to really get into the physical action of it.

Despite, Alice's increasingly outrageous stage performances, it was really Glen Buxton who was becoming the most unpredictable member of the band. I particularly remember this one incident, I guess it must have been around the end of 1969. We were staying at this really funky hotel, as was common in those days for us all to be sleeping in the same room with all our guitars and stuff. One night we were all totally exhausted and went to sleep, and somebody let themselves into the room and they grabbed Glen's guitar and took off. After this, we decided to check out of this hotel and move to a different one.

At the next hotel, we'd left all of our stuff in the lobby near the elevator. We went back across the street to collect the rest of our gear and when we got back somebody had stolen Glen's suitcase. So now Glen has no guitars, no clothes, no identity. At that point he had just lost everything — his sound, his look were all gone. It sounds strange, but from that moment on Glen was never the same. He just never got it all back completely, more or less he was shot down — devastated. It was touch and go from then on.

You have to remember that this was a guy, who even when he was in high school in Arizona, was already drinking a quart of whiskey a day. When I first joined the band, he had been kicked out of his freshman year at college for drinking. Also, at the risk of getting too psychoanalytical, I believe he'd had some relationship problems with his mother and that might have affected him. I remember some nights he'd meet these girls, take them back to the hotel, and make them scream and weird stuff. I don't know what he was doing in there — it sounded really dysfunctional.

On the road, Glen was the one who always attracted the straighter looking women — schoolteacher look-a-likes. Apparently, following an encounter with Glen they were never quite the same again! Not that all the attention was from women. With our looks, outrageous clothes and make-up, it was inevitable that we were getting attention from guys as well. It was kind of an odd situation, because despite our appearance, all the group were heterosexual, beer swilling, all American guys.

I was always a little bit concerned about the whole transvestite image, especially when we played in California. In San Francisco, around the time of the first couple of albums, we would get all these guys following us around. In particular I remember this one guy with really curly hair who was always following Glen all over the place. It was really getting on Glen's nerves. So one time, we were in this hotel and this guy knocks on the door. "Hi Glen", he says and comes in with some of his friends. A couple of hours go by and we really wanted to get rid of them. Finally Glen gets up and goes into the bathroom and says to this guy, "Come here", and the guy follows him into the bathroom. Then Glen says "get into the bathtub", so he does real excited, like something sexual was going to happen. Then Glen turns on the cold water from the shower and soaks this guy. I'll never forget this guy crying out, "Glen, you're the devil…"

Easy Action — Love It To Death

By the time we started working on our second album *Easy Action* we still didn't have a real producer. Then Shep and Joe met David Briggs who had produced Neil Young's Crazy Horse. So we decided to give him a shot at doing our next album. We recorded it at Sunwest studios on Sunset Boulevard, Hollywood. I remember it was the same studio where Rick Nelson and the Stone Canyon Band recorded "Garden Party".

Shep and Joe had also met with the DMA booking agency and Dave Leone said they could get some gigs for us out in the mid-west. That's where we met Leo Fenn who was managing Suzie Quatro and the Pleasure Seekers. As a result we started playing a lot of gigs out in the mid-west area and that's when things really started to pick up for us. During the recording of the album, we went and played a gig in Denver, Colorado. I think this may well have been the famous gig when Alice put his high school cross country training to good use by jumping off stage, running round the stadium's race track, jumping back on stage and finishing the song.

Somehow, once we were outside of the LA music scene, our stage theatrics were met with a much more favourable reaction. Perhaps in LA we had become too associated with the freak scene that surrounded Frank Zappa. Or maybe kids in the mid-west had less preconceived notions about what was hip and fashionable. They sensed that we were a band that could entertain them, and not just another bunch of guys in blue jeans and T-shirts rehashing endless blues jams.

When we got back to LA we found that all our stuff had been moved out the house in the Hollywood Hills where we had all been living. It turned out our rent money had never been passed on to the owner of the house by this maggot landlord. Also, we didn't get on too well with the owner after Alice supposedly went out one night and got real drunk with him and the owner of the house tried to get it on with him. But in a lot respects we weren't sad to be out of LA because the whole LA scene wasn't really helping the band to take root and develop musically, and especially financially.

My opinion is that we were really rushed into the *Easy Action* album which was released in June 1970. Nevertheless, we all felt that it was a big improvement on *Pretties For You* in both the songwriting and production departments. But it was apparent to us that we needed to get further away from the reason why Zappa had signed us in the first place. We were worried that a lot of people just thought we were just an extension of Frank's dark sense of humour and satire. We saw the funnier elements within our music as being more surrealistic than comic.

As a result, a lot of time was spent discussing the direction the band should be taking. At this time we did everything together, we were still very much "a band" making band decisions. Every detail was looked at. We were even painstaking about picking out the lettering for the album's front cover.

Of the songs on the album, "Mr and Misdemeanor" was generally considered to be the best track. It was typical of a lot of songs that we used to write around that time that were based around a play on words. "Still No Air" demonstrated how we were all still hung up on *West Side Story*. We all dug that gang thing — you know, that *Clockwork Orange*-type of scenario. "Refrigerator Heaven" was our Beatles trip. We used the reference "feel like a BB On Mars" from the first album. I sang lead vocal on "Below Your Means" and "Beautiful Flyaway" — the latter was a kind of a meditation song, sort of my attempt at being George Harrison. "Return Of The Spiders" was dedicated to Gene Vincent as we had backed him in Toronto.

"Lay Down And Die Goodbye" was the same song that dated back to the days when we were calling ourselves The Nazz — so this was really our second stab at it. In the middle of the song we inserted the segment where you hear this voice saying, "If you don't like what we say you have a choice, you can

turn us off". That was from a tape David Briggs had of Tommy Smothers from the Smothers Brothers Show. It seemed oddly appropriate. After all, we were still being quite successful at turning some people off.

In late 1970, we finally decided that our career in LA was pretty much going nowhere. Our first two LPs for Zappa's label had been only moderately successful, and the relationship with Straight had never really worked out like either party had expected. According to some sources we were $100,000 unrecouped. As a result Zappa's manager and Straight label boss, Herb Cohen, decided to recover his losses by selling the label, including our band, to Warner Bros who were handling Straight's distribution. (The publishing part of this agreement was to become the subject of a later legal dispute.)

I think Warner Bros paid about $50,000 for Straight's whole roster of acts. By this time this included Linda Ronstadt, who was in the Stone Ponies, and also James Taylor who was in another of the groups. I think Warners really wanted both of them because they very much represented the type of music that was popular at that time. They got the Alice Cooper group as a weird kind of bonus. Considering the number of records we all went on to sell, it must have been one of the all time bargains!

Having been forced out of our Hollywood home, it was agreed that as we were making considerable inroads in the mid-west, it would make sense to move to Alice's hometown of Detroit. The net result was that we were now signed to Warner Bros and our "headquarters" moved to a farm outside of Detroit. It was here that we started working on material for our third album. To celebrate our move, for our first show in Detroit we rolled these car tires around the stage which we had sprayed silver and gold. After all, this was Detroit — motor city. In the beginning, we had this guy who was going to supply us with props and his deal was that he was just going to spray every-thing silver, that was his idea, a silver telephone, a silver lamp, we used to joke about this guy, we thought it was funny.

The farm was in Pontiac, Michigan and comprised of a small farmhouse, a big barn and some 50 acres of land. Again it was a communal type of set-up, but within that set-up we all pretty much had rooms to ourselves. We con-verted the room off the kitchen for Glen, as he tended to make the most noise. I remember hearing this girl of his called Moira screaming all through the house. Summer at the farm was particularly nice because it had a little pool. However, we could only use this for a short period because it was so cold up there that it was frozen over most of the year. Most importantly, we had a big room out the back where we could write and rehearse and that's where we wrote a lot of the new material.

Things were pretty basic out at the farm. There was this well that would always lose its prime because the head needed a new gasket. It was really awful. If you drank that water first thing in the morning, you'd end up running to the bathroom to throw up because there was so much iron in it.

This guy would come over and re-prime the well. Instead of changing the gasket he'd just dig a little deeper and bring the water level up. We thought he

was funny, because we'd never seen such a redneck before. He'd come over and get drunk and go stomping and dancing around the living room and we'd be clapping along and laughing at him — it was pretty sick. Alice later recorded a song on one of his albums called "Ubangi Stomp" which was Dennis' nickname for this guy's dance. Also, it was at the farm that Cindy Smith (Neal's sister) and Dennis became an item. It turned out later they had gotten married and not told anybody.

Also, we could have outrageous parties at the farm. Some of the Detroit people would come over, The Stooges, MC5, SRC Scott Richard's band. Certainly there were some comparisons between us and the Detroit bands like The Stooges and the MC5. I don't think it's so much a case of what came first but just generally what was going on at the time. With The Stooges the rest of the band stood there with their Nazi stuff, and Iggy was the whole show, it was kind of the same with Alice. I don't know how much Iggy drank, but Alice certainly drank to do that outrageousness on stage. With Iggy it just came natural, I think he was just very, very strange.

I remember one particular time back in early 1970, we all went to see Iggy at the Whiskey in LA. He was jumping around on the tables and he had this candle that had all this hot wax in it, so being Iggy he proceeded to pour all this hot wax down his chest. All I can really remember about the MC5 was their lead singer, Rob Tyner, with that huge afro, sweating like a pig.

Certainly once we got out of California and into the mid-west and the Detroit scene, people picked up on the fact that there was more to the band than just being seen as a bunch of transvestites. We all had really super long hair, so that was one thing, but I think people realised we were doing something different from a lot of bands, so we just kind of went with it. In a lot of ways, Detroit was a much more natural setting for the band than LA had been. With its violent overtones, our show was more suited to middle America than the laid back attitude of the West Coast. Detroit was a violent place with drug dealers hanging around on every street corner. Alice told a journalist at the time, "They don't just mess around in Detroit, they go... all the way. And it gets to you". Also, I think Dennis was probably right when he said, "We get off more on a Detroit-type crowd — crowds that get physically into a concert".

Certainly some people considered what we were doing to be in bad taste. But our view was that everybody could get what they wanted out of it. When

GOOSE LAKE INTERNATIONAL MUSIC FESTIVAL
AUGUST 7-8-9 FRI SAT SUN

FRIDAY

SMALL FACES • TEN YEARS AFTER • CHICAGO
JOHN SEBASTIAN • N.Y. ROCK&ROLL ENSEMBLE • SRC • MIGHTY
QUICK • JOHN DRAKE SHAKEDOWN

SATURDAY

JETHRO TULL • MOUNTAIN • FLYING BURRITO BROTHERS
LITTER • STOOGES • 3ʳᵈ POWER • BROWNSVILLE STATION

SUNDAY

JETHRO TULL • SAVAGE GRACE • FLOCK • JAMES GANG
ALICE COOPER • SUITE CHARITY • DETROIT FEATURING MITCH RYDER
BOB SEGER SYSTEM • FROST

FACILITIES

GOOSE LAKE PARK is a PERMANENT festival site, the first of its kind. Permanent rest rooms with FREE SHOWERS, paved roads, plenty of FREE PARKING on the grounds, FREE CAMPING with free firewood and plastic sheeting in case of rain, and FREE SWIMMING. Food is available from concession stands over the entire site at LOW PRICES, and FREE FOOD is available from 2 kitchens, one staffed by OPEN CITY open 24 hours. A grocery and drug store will also be available. TWO MEDICAL TEAMS will be on the site, one staffed by OPEN CITY. An entire meadow has been reserved for MOVEMENT GROUPS to set up literature tables. Another meadow is reserved for BIKERS. Everything possible is being done to provide for the PEOPLE'S NEEDS while attending the GOOSE LAKE MUSIC FESTIVAL. We welcome your suggestions and criticisms !!!!

Tickets are available by advance sale only and are $15 for 3 days.
Tickets may be purchased at Goose Lake office after July 29th.
OUTLETS: Detroit: Hudson's and Grinnell's - Chicago: All Ticketron outlets.
Cincinnati: N.Y. Times clothing store - Toledo: Grinnell's
Columbus: Central ticket office and Sears.

 BY MAIL: Send a self-addressed envelope to: Goose Lake Park, Inc.
30999 Ten Mile Rd., Farmington, Mich. 48024
Mail order must be received by July 29th. money orders only.
A one day only chit, good only Sunday is available at all
outlets for $6. No re-admittance once you leave the park.
Goose Lake Park, Jackson, Mich.
Take I-94 to Race Road exit and follow the signs.

people came to our show they didn't only want to hear the music, they also wanted to watch something. They weren't there to see the type of musicianship exemplified by Eric Clapton or Jimi Hendrix, they were there to see some action. Early on, as I said we would just do anything to get people's attention. We would be playing the music and Alice would pretty much ad-lib his way

through. Later on, the whole show became much more planned and choreographed.

After we moved to the farm, Shep Gordon approached Nimbus 9 Productions in Toronto to produce the next LP. Nimbus 9 was Jack Richardson and his up-and-coming assistant (alias the boy wonder) Bob Ezrin. We felt a new sense of hope for our next album because Richardson was a seasoned veteran with several hits under his belt with Canadian acts like The Guess Who.

So, we decided to record *Love It To Death* at the RCA building in Chicago and Bob Ezrin would be the producer with Jack Richardson as executive producer. In terms of the songwriting, it was clear a change needed to be made and I pushed for the songs to be credited as individual writers rather than the group as a whole. I also wanted to have a little more say about what was going on in the songs. Our personal styles had started to emerge and it was plain to see who was best suited for the different aspects of the group's music. I thought there was plenty of room to accommodate everyone's taste and playing styles so as not to create any problems. Dennis didn't really like that because he wanted every song to be a band effort. But I felt that this was the reason the songs weren't being developed properly. Also, we had done the first two albums as a "band effort" and they hadn't been that successful, so what was the point in repeating that formula again? I was hoping that with Bob Ezrin we'd found somebody good enough who could really "produce" the album and develop the music.

Which is pretty much what happened, although it wasn't all plain sailing. I remember while we were living in Detroit, Bob Ezrin would come out and visit us at the farm. I remember during one of his visits me and him got into this big argument. There's a segment in the Alice Cooper *Prime Cuts* video where Bob talks about the push and pull between him and myself in the early days which really developed the Alice Cooper sound. I think that was typical of the differences of opinion we had.

Essentially, Bob thought much of the music wasn't melodic enough. He was a classically trained pianist and he started working out all these classical parts for the songs. I'd say to him, "Bob, you know we're not Procol Harum. We're a live rock 'n' roll a band who eat little babies — you know — we're real treacherous and spooky. You can't put stuff in the music that's not us!"

Eventually I got fed up with what he was doing to several of the songs and I would say things like, "Bob that's way too much — you're going over the line."

55

It got to the point where every song was winding up with a classical part. OK, so it worked well on something like "Second Coming", where Alice had the initial idea based around this line that he had written "time is getting closer, I read it on the poster". Bob then added the piano piece.

Sometimes he would sit and play me all kinds of stuff at the piano. I respected him because he knew his music. But I think Bob always assumed that I was the one in the group who was a pain in the ass to deal with. Alice had no problem with Bob. Dennis too just went along with most things, for the most part he would never say what he really felt. Glen was becoming increasingly oblivious to it all. He was always going, "that's fine, whatever you guys decide". So, it was left to me to stand up to Bob.

What annoyed me was that Bob seemed to have the impression that the group was musically inferior and he was somehow musically superior. Apparently, there was even this running joke at Nimbus 9 — "Whoever fucks up, has to produce the Alice Cooper group". Even back then, I always got the distinct impression that Joe and Shep thought the band was just there to write songs and back Alice. Later, I think Shep and Bob Ezrin felt that they could manufacture that sound without us — well in my opinion they were proved wrong.

In any event there was considerable friction between Bob and me — a lot of competition between us. I remember this came to a head when we were sitting in the studio recording the "Mommy where's Daddy" section of "Dwight Frye". On the record we got a girl friend of ours, Monica, to speak the "Mommy where's daddy....." bit. She had this real baby-type voice. (I used to say it when we played live). Bob was playing this piano piece which I wrote and Brian the engineer came over and said to him, "That was really beautiful". Bob never went out of his way to tell anyone that I wrote that piano part. I mean I only played it every fucking night live. So I turned to the engineer and said, "Thank you — I wrote that." Well the whole room got real quiet and I got up and left. I guess I might have acted like an ass, but I was proud of our music and what we had accomplished.

"Dwight Frye" was essentially about this guy who's a mental patient. The repeated vocal line "I wanna get outta here" was of course a reference to the mental institution that poor Dwight had been put in. The vocal was recorded in the studio with Alice caged in a structure of folding chairs so as to give him the feeling of claustrophobia.

Also, when we played "Dwight Frye" live, a nurse would come out and bring Alice back on stage wearing a straight jacket. Once when we were playing up in Canada, somehow we managed to lose the straight jacket. Of course, the good old Canadians had outlawed straight jackets many years ago, so it was impossible to find a replacement. In the end we had to have one flown up from the States — naturally Americans are always good for a straight jacket or two!

I really liked the groove on "Long Way To Go" — Bob did play the piano part on that one! We stuck the line "I guess I'll love it — I love it to death" in there. Alice turned round and said, "Yeh, 'Love it to death man' is a real hip term in LA right now". So we used the phrase for the album title as well.

"Is It My Body" was a song I wrote at the cheesy motel in New York where Glen had his stuff stolen from. It was about all the fans who were now turning on to us — at the time it felt a bit like there were these vultures sitting at every corner and here we were, the fresh meat being trucked into town. My response was, "We're here and we've got to show them what we've got" — as the lyrics go, "what have I got that makes you want to love me...". For the live version we included the middle section that went, "going to the boneyard...." Again, these were typical horror movie-type lyrics accompanied by a slow plodding drumbeat from Neal.

Neal wrote "Hallowed Be They Name" and I really liked that song. He wrote the guitar part sort of horizontally. I remember Bob Ezrin "ordered" me to learn the song in a different key, I didn't really understand why he wanted me to, and I kind of resented it. I thought he was being difficult just for the sake of it. But apparently, the RCA building in Chicago is nothing but a giant receiver. All the radio airwaves came to that building. So when I played the Farfisa organ for the song in the original key, it was picking up all these radio waves. Anyway, I carried on playing the song the way I had learned it, and Bob said to me, "I thought I told you to play it in that other key", and I said, "Aahh, you go ahead and play it, you need the work anyway". So, he ended up playing it.

I remember Dennis got real upset because my organ part to "Black Juju" was similar to Pink Floyd's "Set The Controls For The Heart Of The Sun". Somebody made reference to this in a review (*Rolling Stone* considered it so similar that, "the Coopers may yet have to answer to the Floyd in court"). I said to him, "Come on Dennis, we are all big Pink Floyd fans — so what, we

got caught on that one". After all, we emulated a lot of groups. The Beatles on *Pretties For You* and *Easy Action* and later the Doors and the Detroit sound.

"Caught In A Dream" was written at the farm. There was this dog that lived in the area but had no real home. It was a black Labrador and Dennis called him Black Juju after our song of the same name. I was out in the field one night walking with the dog and the line, "Running through the world with a gun in my back, trying to catch a ride in a Cadillac" sort of just came to me. I could see highway 1-75 from where I was and the cars were zooming by. The opening riff I had written years before that as part of a different song and was originally much slower. Looking back on all this today, I feel that the writing, the putting it all together, no matter who wrote what, was the greatest joy and sort of a labour of love for me.

"Sun Arise" was a version of the sixties hit by Rolf Harris, a great tune to end the album with, but we used to open the live shows with it.

An issue concerning the cover to the LP was really the first time we had to deal with album censorship, but not the last. On the original *Love It To Death* album cover Alice had his thumb sticking out from under his cape in a phallic way. Anyway, this was in 1971 when Spiro Agnew was on the rampage about drugs and censorship, so there was pressure put on Warner Bros to change the cover because the thumb looked like a penis. So Warner Bros, fearful of upsetting anyone, airbrushed it out.

For the first few albums the band tended to come up with the album cover concepts — even though Alive Productions (Joe and Shep) were sometimes credited with them, which isn't strictly true. The inside sleeve of *Love It To Death* was a good example. We took those pictures out at the farm, we were probably bored and needed something to do — Joe and Shep weren't even around. The band photo inside Alice's eyes was taken through a fish-eyed lens in the farm's big horse paddock.

When *Love It To Death* was released in February 1971, our hopes that it would be a considerable improvement on its predecessors were realised. We had no real desire to remain a "cult" band with a small following and we genuinely wanted to break out of the underground and make an impact on a greater number of people. It was clear from the opening bars of *Love It To Death* that Bob Ezrin's classical inclination mixed with our raw rock 'n' roll attitude was beginning to produce a new distinctive band sound. In places sophisticated and orchestral, on other songs hard driving rock music.

Above: Playing the Orange County Pop Festival,
Orange County Fairground, California.
Below: Alice ands Neal share press coverage with
some fans at the same festival.

We were even beginning to receive fan mail like, "I've never been affected by anything like I was by you. The first time I heard *Love It To Death* I couldn't sleep for four days I was so excited". More worryingly, one guy even sent us a plastic bag full of his semen. It seemed we were yet to entirely shrug off that sexual interest from guys. I think we were the type of band that attracted a lot of lost souls. When we met them they would tell us, "You're music started it all for me, got me going", or "My dad hates you because he thinks you're fags. Shit on him." They were the kind of people who didn't know how to fit in, whether it was sexually or whatever. I suppose our show being kind of freaky and violent provided a focus for them to vent their feelings. They didn't have a clue. So we created a new pigeon hole for them.

I don't think the critics lost quite so much sleep over *Love It To Death* as some of the fans obviously had, but the reviews were generally more positive about our new record. *Rolling Stone* said that, "A lot will like *Love It To Death*, especially those with an ear for nicely wrought mainstream punk raunch and snidely clever lyrics." In any event, it didn't much matter what the critics thought, by April the first single off the album, "I'm Eighteen", had hit the US charts.

"I'm Eighteen" came from a jam based around the phrase "I wish I was 18 again". I remember we were jamming on it and Alice suddenly sang "And I like it!" The lyrics originally were, "Be my only high school queen, be the only one, I wish I was 18 again". I remember Alice showed the band the lyrics he had written and we sat there and said, "These are great lyrics, but we all feel you can write some even better, go back and rewrite them". So he went back and wrote a second version and he's going, "Yeh, this is it". Again we felt, "Better, but not there yet". The third time we said, "Yeh, right on". He did it. He took all the ideas and lyrics that had been floating around and hit the nail on the head. We wanted a hit record, now we were pretty sure we had what we had been looking for.

"I'm Eighteen" was a classic rock 'n' roll teenage anthem. Writing a song about being eighteen seemed very appropriate to us at the time. The basic idea was for Alice to sing about a confused teenager's apparent malaise about his tender years, until you are hit with the "And I like it" line, implying that the song might be about a confused teenager, but fuck everybody else, he was still going to enjoy being alive too.

One of the stories about how the track became a hit was that CLKW radio in Ontario was playing the song all the time. Being the most popular station in Detroit, it was broadcast from Cleveland to Toronto and beyond. At the time the Canadian government had just introduced a ruling whereby a percentage of music played on Canadian stations had to be produced by home grown talent. Having two Canadian producers, Jack Richardson and Bob Ezrin, "I'm Eighteen" was generally considered to have enough of a Canadian input to satisfy this ruling. Later it was changed so that the actual artist had to be Canadian, but by this time it was too late, "I'm Eighteen" was a hit. As a result of the single's success, *Love It To Death* reached number 35 on the US charts. It seemed at last that things were happening for us.

Another version of the story goes that, unbeknownst to the band at the time, Leo Fenn slept with the program director from CKLW radio and that broke the record. Another reason might be that we had built up a phone bill a mile long — "Hello, can you please play the new Alice Cooper record, 'I'm 18'?" — you can imagine the sort of thing, we all had raw fingers from all that dialling! We would get everyone we knew to call and request it. Shep even hired people for a dollar a call, from what I understood.

The record company, however, took their time to catch up with our sudden success. When we went on the road in May 1971 to promote the LP, we'd show up in the towns where the song was on heavy rotation on the radio and there would be no product in the stores. It was clear that Warner Bros hadn't gotten behind it yet, so Shep flew out to LA ready to kill. I guess he jumped down their throats because the next week there was a life size cardboard cutout of Alice in the stores and plenty of *Love It To Death* albums in the racks.

These cardboard figures had Alice's distinctive dark black eye make-up and looked real intimidating. By now Alice had started to apply his trademark black dark spider's web circles around his eyes. He had picked up the idea from a brochure for the Alvin Ali dance troupe which featured these clowns wearing this bizarre make-up. Alice thought that was real cool and eventually it became a regular part of his stage look.

We were also forever looking for more intimidating imagery to use live. After the straight jacket segment for "Dwight Frye", the electric chair just seemed like the next logical step. We built the electric chair out at the farm, and the idea was that we would use it during "Black Juju". At the point in the song where we all went, "Wake up, wake up", Alice would then get elec-

trocuted. It was a nice touch. Of course later we progressed to the gallows for "Killer". I guess the electric chair could have resurfaced because not many people got to see it. We could have had big electros shooting out everywhere like something out of a Frankenstein movie! Just a thought.

The *Love It To Death* tour finished in the US in the early Autumn. In October it was time to take our brand of music further afield and we embarked on a short tour of Europe which took in Denmark, Holland and England.

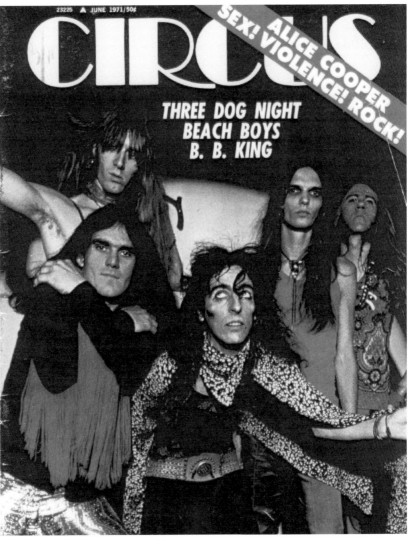

Above: A healthy, wholesome look is important to any group!

Killer

Originally we had two different ideas for the cover of *Killer*. At first the album was going to be called "Killer / Convicted". That particular idea was taken from the US TV detective series *Elliot Ness*. The opening sequence features a news truck which would come around the corner and a stack of newspapers would be sent spinning off the back. Then they would eventually stop spinning around to reveal the big story of the day. We were going to have a view from the truck — a close up of the sidewalk, the newsboy with his hat and bag and the news-stand in the back. There would be a stack of newspapers in a bundle with the covers saying "Killer / Convicted" with Alice's picture underneath. But at the time it was too complicated a picture to shoot properly. We didn't have Drew of Pacific Eye & Ear then. He was the guy who ended up doing the drawings for the *Greatest Hits* album. Later he went on to do the posters for Hollywood movies like *Indiana Jones*.

We still didn't have a large budget for the cover even though the band was really rolling. By that time we'd picked up a solid following and we'd either blow the other band off the stage, or leave such an impression on everybody that it was impossible to ignore us. We were also starting to get great reviews, much bigger gigs, and more money. One time we were playing some gigs in Florida and this girl gave Neal a boa constrictor and he started to carry it on tour with him. It then struck us that it would be a neat idea to use the snake on the cover. I guess it came from the bible — that whole good and evil bit.

Maybe the cover of *Killer* was sort of a premonition because eventually Alice started using it in the show.

Initially I think Alice was a bit wary about performing with the reptile, who by now had been christened Kachina. But it was just this sort of reaction that we liked about incorporating it into the show. Producing a snake in public always causes a reaction of some sort, whether it be revulsion, fascination, even sexual stimulation. Anyway, we managed to persuade Alice to overcome his inhibitions and the snake was soon a regular feature at our live shows. I guess it was an image that grew to be synonymous with the group, and Alice's live performance in particular. During "Be My Lover" he would appear to coax and tease the snake, other times it was lovingly wrapped around his body or head. In any event, it seemed a natural decision to use a close-up of Kachina for the cover of the *Killer* LP.

It was typical of the way everything in our career just evolved in that kind of way — from the make-up on *Love It To Death*, through to the electric chair and then the gallows. The snake was really just another step toward the scary macabre thing the band could generate with the right show. But we would also improvise with any props that would cause a reaction. I remember one time we were playing somewhere in the South and my aunt came to see us. In the back of this theatre there was a big wooden cross painted white. That night during one of our jams Alice gets the cross and puts it on his back. He then does the Jesus walk to the stage. Well for months I heard about that from my aunt — she thought it was so weird and blasphemous. I told her, "Hey, it was there, we didn't bring it with us. It was just part of that particular performance, so what's the problem?"

In terms of record company support, everything was on a much better footing now that we had completely severed ties with Bizarre and Straight. As the shows and records became more successful, Warner Bros started to get a hundred percent behind us. As a result *Killer* became what *Love It To Death* had wanted to be. We had this distinct feeling that the music on *Killer* was unique and very different from what many other bands were producing.

"Under My Wheels" was written when Leo Fenn came to work for us. We were in Michigan somewhere and we had a layover for a week — no gigs. We must have still been pretty poor, because I can remember sitting around eating crackers and cheese and bread. Well Dennis had this riff "telephone is ringing" stop "you got me on the run" stop, etc. So we worked together on that one.

Bob Ezrin worked out those great horn arrangements — a very Mitch Ryder and Detroit Wheels type of groove.

"Be My Lover" was a song I wrote about this girl Chip — she was the sister of Ashley Pandel, our PR guy. They were from Michigan and she hung around a lot. Once she came walking into the room we were rehearsing in and I sort of wrote this as it happened — "She struts into the room, Well I don't know her". This was the first time I ever wrote like that. The second verse came from a conversation I had with some old lady I was sitting next to on the plane on the way to our next show. I told her that, "I came from Detroit City and played guitar in a long haired rock n' roll band". I tried to explain why the band was named Alice Cooper — hence the line, "She asked me why the singer's name was Alice". I finally gave up by saying, "you really wouldn't understand".

Alice added that burlesque ending to "Be My Lover", pushing that sexual thing. At first the ending seemed a bit contrived to me — that whole Mae West "come up and see me some time" impersonation kind of bugged me — but eventually I got over it. And yes, Neal did drop his sticks at the end — sorry Neal. (The sound of Neal Smith dropping his sticks is clearly audible after the first drum roll ending).

Also at the very end of the track there's that fast backwards section where the song seems to end abruptly. Well, I wanted it to end on the last guitar note and asked Bob Ezrin about it. Bob and me were still having these flare-ups. So he said, "No, let's leave it the way it is. It will take too much time to set it all back up again and re-edit", and I said, "Well that's why I mentioned it *while* you were still editing". That also kind of bugged me — but it still worked. And then I grew up and became mature! Not!

"Halo Of Flies" was actually an amalgamation of several unfinished songs I had written which we then strung together. The first part was originally called "The More I Want To Know You". Alice added the line with the melody from Rogers and Hammerstein's "My Favourite Things" later. The riff after Alice sings "flies" was from another song altogether. When we were at the Shore Crest Hotel in Detroit, on Woodward Drive, Cindy Lang (Alice's girlfriend) came up with the title. It was supposed to be our 'progressive' song. We wanted to use it as a vehicle to show the band's versatility. During live shows Neal would have his drum solo in the middle and I used quite a bit of wah-wah. Not just any wah-wah mind you — there's a story behind that....

Above: Alice and Neal gone fishing.
Alice nursing his ever-present tin of Budweiser.
Photo: Torn Ticket Productions

Years back, when we were at a Mothers' rehearsal, during a break I had switched my Voxx pedal for Frank Zappa's wah-wah pedal because I thought his sounded better. Sorry Frank, wherever you are. Then sometime later Les Braiden, who worked with Pink Floyd, got us tickets to see Cream. We got backstage and met Jack Bruce. I smoked a bunch of joints with him and listened to some roughs from the *Wheels Of Fire* album. I also met Eric Clapton and liked the sound of Eric's wah-wah pedal better than Zappa's. Well, being the young, foolish kid I was, I switched Frank Zappa's wah-wah pedal with Eric Clapton's — sorry Eric. But as fate would have it someone eventually repossessed it from me... And that's a true story.

Bob Ezrin continued to add this classical edge to some of the music. He did some real lush string arrangements on "Desperado". The guitar riff actually came from a piece I used to tune up on. Dennis, Alice, and I all contributed to the lyrics. Again, there was real teamwork on that one.

In contrast, "You Drive Me Nervous" was another of the LP's driving rock songs, while "Yeah, Yeah, Yeah", displayed the continuing influence of British r&b, complete with Alice adding a distinctive harmonica solo in the middle.

"Dead Babies" was adapted from a song that had been around since the days of The Spiders. We all wrote that. At rehearsals Alice used to read us articles out of the newspapers. I remember him recounting two articles about this little girl who ate something poisonous and died as a result — it wasn't aspirin like in the song. So we wrote a song about a girl called little Betty who over-dosed on aspirin. It was a song about child neglect and abuse. The "Goodbye little Betty" part, complete with the Beatle-ish horn arrangement, was written in the studio with Bob Ezrin.

Once we had "Be My Lover", "Desperado" and "Dead Babies" all finished, there seemed to be a really dark element to the new songs. Although I wrote most of the lighter material, I used to dig that dark side to our sound. I would listen to a lot of B-movie horror soundtracks, and also John Barry's James Bond soundtracks. We wanted to come up with a theme song for the album, so one night when everyone else was out, Dennis and I had planned to take some peyote a friend had given us. We went into the backroom at the farm in Michigan and tried to think about what would be the most intense thing we could write. We tried to work ourselves into a really dark mood, we talked about when you know you're going to die — what is the scariest thing about that? What would the waiting be like? So we wrote the title song "Killer". When we recorded the song we used a Moog synthesizer for the first time to make that noise at the very end of the album that sounds like a swarm of bees.

By this time we were playing a lot of gigs around the mid-west — Ohio, Michigan, and Illinois. Anyway, we were at Chicago's O'Hare airport and there was a four-hour layover. We got to talking with Leo Fenn about what to do for the next tour to accompany the track "Killer". We decided we would like to try to make people feel the dark mood that Dennis and I had conjured up on the album. Someone suggested the idea of hanging Alice on stage. We instantly took to the idea, especially with us coming from Arizona, it seemed kind of appropriate. After all Arizona has a history of a lot of hangings — out West it was called frontier justice. In all the Western movies there'd always be a gallows. It was a natural extension from the previous electric chair idea. If it was a step backwards in the history of capital punishment, it was a step forward for us in presentation. Obviously, the electrocution idea had been a bit difficult to fake. With a hanging it seemed like there was an opportunity to be a bit more slick in its execution — if you'll pardon the pun!

We had been using props for a long time and it became a real theatrical goal. But we would use anything. When we performed "Dead Babies" we had baby dolls and Alice would stab them with a sword. We would also throw out baby doll parts into the audience. I used to have a doll's arm on the vibrato bar of my Gibson SG. One day I just picked up this baby's arm which was strewn around the stage and attached it to my guitar.

The gallows section to the stage show was based specifically around the songs on *Killer*. First of all, during "Dead Babies". Alice would rip a baby doll apart and then smear fake blood over his mouth like he was some kind of child serial killer. Alice would just tear those things apart. He would joke in interviews that he had nothing against kids as such, it was just a hatred of dolls that went back to his childhood.

Then during a sequence of dry ice and claps of thunder, the rest of the band would carry these lighted torches which was an image similar to the 'raiding Frankenstein's castle' idea. Glen would lead Alice out to the gallows like something right out of a Hollywood horror movie. Our shows always had that good and evil theme — crime and punishment. If you were bad you got punished. Despite our bad boys of rock reputation, there was a real moral aspect to our shows. The bad guy always got his just punishment.

We began to refer to the different parts of the show as the "white set" and the "dark set". The show would start out light and then get dark after the execution. At the end it was, boom!, and back to the light again, or rebirth if your prefer. It was supposed to be a big showbiz ending. That was always the basic formula right from the beginning. At the end of the show Alice would re-emerge to spray the front row with beer and dollar bills. I remember one reviewer putting it, "This makes everything American: American as TV, violence, sexual confusion; vulgarity, the Almighty Dollar". Alice's own father also put it rather succinctly at the time, "He's a pretty good ham on stage".

We got Warner Bros to build us this large gallows that could be folded away. We explained to them that we wanted something that we could fit into 5 or 6 anvil road cases. So they designed it. There was the upper structure, the staircase, the flooring, the trapdoor. For the hanging sequence Alice would wear this vest with the hooks in the back. In the end Alice wore the vest for the whole set — it looked good with all those rivets in it.

Underneath, he would wear a black body stocking with holes torn in it. This harness had a crotch with belts strapped on it so it would hold your body from

Above: Shep Gordon tears his hair out over the logistics of the 1972 *Killer* tour.
Photo: Michael Bruce (Torn Ticket Productions)

the jerk of the fall — so as to avoid breaking any arms and legs. It was rigged in a way that you couldn't get hung — although think of the publicity if we really hung Alice on stage! We would have been beyond legendary — they would say "that Alice Cooper, he was well hung." (Just a joke folks).

By the time of *Killer* we were really co-ordinating the music in with the live show. It was much more of a stage musical mixed with rock 'n' roll. Gone were the days when we played the music and Alice improvised and ad-libbed in front of us. As we became more aware of the effect we could have on an audience so we worked up the idea of a sort of rock 'n' roll theatre.

From *Killer* onwards we really meticulously staged the shows — we were big planners. We'd sit and talk until we were blue in the face about the shows and the music. We really cared about the music at that point. We were becoming a show business, road-hardened, working machine. We really were. From the end of *Love It To Death* through *Killer* to *School's Out* then to the big show based on *Billion Dollar Babies* we really felt we were progressing toward producing the ultimate show, perfecting the art of live performance.

There was no doubt that the pressure was increasing. As the demand grew, so we were doing more and more travelling. But we got very business-like about it all. Although there was a lot of drinking and joking around, everyone had their job to do. Alice would go down to the local radio station while we sound-checked. We all shared equally in the band. It had taken us quite a while to get to where we were and we were enjoying it. The bottom line was to always to put on the best possible show no matter what the obstacles.

I think everything was really on an even keel within the band at the time of *Killer*. There was an intricate balance between what the different members of the band were doing — really in the gung-ho spirit of a group. Looking back on it, what *Killer* achieved was a balance of all the different elements within the band; my pop melodies, Alice's menacing lyrics and Bob Ezrin's orchestration. The end result was a finely balanced record.

Also, although Alice was doing his thing as the spokesperson, he had yet to go too far out on a limb of his own. Glen hadn't gotten too carried away with his drinking and he was still functioning. I wasn't at the point where I was dissatisfied and wanted to do some solo stuff. Dennis was still very much into the band. We also still had Charlie Carnel. Charlie was our light show guy who had stuck with us from our days in Phoenix. He was very close with Dennis. On the albums Charlie would get a credit as "environmental control". He was really considered to be the sixth member of the Alice Cooper group.

Killer was released in November 1971 and reached No 21 in the US charts (*Love It To Death* was also still in the top 100 at the time). In the UK it reached No 27. The upbeat reviews continued and coverage for the band in the press was generally on an upward spiral. Even Lester Bangs, who at one time or another had been less than complimentary about us, described *Killer* as "one of the finest rock 'n' roll records of 1971".

We were eventually presented with a gold disc for the LP's sales at Warner Bros' offices in Burbank. But when we turned up for the photo session, the gold discs hadn't arrived, so closer inspection reveals that all the band are in fact holding copies of Jimi Hendrix's *Rainbow Bridge*.

The *Killer* road show with the hanging sequence was such a success that we toured it almost continually from December 1971 right through to May 1972. It was like a non-stop party. It was a lot of hard work but it was always fun.

School's Out

As the group became more successful, so everything started moving so quickly that it was all flying past in a blur. The *Killer* road show had garnered a lot of press reaction and there was even more demand for us to play. As a result, in the spring we didn't have a long time to record the *School's Out* album. We were always playing or something. So we actually had to come up with material very quickly. If Dennis didn't have the germ of a musical idea, or I didn't have something, then Bob Ezrin would come up with an idea. We were a very creative unit. Despite time constraints, Bob was always very particular about the recording. Everything was very clean — we were all learning to have very good studio techniques. Bob worked very hard on the production of *School's Out*. Despite our odd relationship, I can't give him enough credit — he really helped us become the success that we were.

We rehearsed hard for both the *School's Out* record and shows at Studio Instrument Rentals of Los Angeles. We had mostly moved back to the West Coast by this time. But really we were moving around so much that we were mostly living out of suitcases, mainly staying in legendary dives like the Landmark Hotel (where Janis Joplin overdosed).

We were now really keen to display the showbiz side of the band. Our fascination with musicals like *West Side Story* was really beginning to influence the shows. Also, Alice was a real TV addict. We all liked the whole idea of a slick presentation. I think Alice wasn't far wrong when he would say in interviews that the Alice Cooper group were really the product of television. Our music and the show had really grown out of our childhood interests and influences. A reporter once described that travelling with us was like a mixture of *200 Motels*, *The Lost Weekend* and *I Love Lucy*.

I think we were an All-American band — violence, TV, the movies, the record industry — we kind of personified the good and bad about America. How someone can go from nothing and make it big. But our take on it was that you always paid in the end, with the indulgence, the back room deals. So, we had a sort of a sarcastic view of American life, admittedly, a little bit on the extreme side. Looking back on those years, with all the struggles and violence that was going on with Vietnam and Watergate and such, I think in a lot of ways we were a very natural part of that.

But contrary to what many believed, Alice was really very straight, other than being a big beer drinker. Alice would always be carrying a Budweiser. "If you ever lose the band", the joke went, "go to the bar, because that's where you'll find them". From the morning until the time we went on stage he might have gone through a case, but he was the kind of guy that just sipped on it and probably didn't finish the whole thing, maybe the beer got warm and then he'd open another one. I think he drank more and more as there was increasing pressure on him to be more outrageous and upstage the last thing he did or said.

But off stage he was not at all the freaky image he liked to portray on stage. Most of the time he used to like to sit and watch TV. I mean how bizarre can you be watching the 150th episode of the *Honeymooners*? It was very boring, in my opinion, to be just sitting there watching TV all the time. I wanted to go out to museums and see the sights. After the shows I wanted to go out and meet some of the audience but that was frowned upon by the rest of the band.

I remember one occasion very early on when we were playing in Seal Beach, California in the late sixties, we were going through a lot of musical changes and I wanted to know how we sounded. So after the show I went out in the crowd and walked around. I think Dick the road manager heard me asking some of the people, "What did you think of the show?" So when I got back into the dressing room, road manager Leo Fenn took me aside and said, "You shouldn't go out and talk to the audience, it's unprofessional", and I said "Bullshit — that's ridiculous". For some odd reason they thought it was

Above: Programme for the band's gig at Wembley's
Empire Pool in June 1972

demeaning. To me these people were the ones who bought our records. Their opinions were important to me. I was the guy writing the songs — so I was trying to get some feedback from our fans.

Contrary to the popular conception, the Alice Cooper group wasn't as big a partying band as some I could mention. We didn't have big riders — just a couple of cases of Budweiser beers and sodas. Usually after the show there would be a party thrown by the road manager or the record company. There would be a lot of food around, we would have food fights with the roadies, the usual stuff. But generally speaking we were trying to hang onto what we were doing, keep our heads together. We were actually pretty quiet a lot of the time.

As regards drugs, at one time or another, everyone tried a little of everything. But generally as we got more and more professional that tapered off. Imagine trying to stage the kind of show we did if everyone was going around tripping all the time. It was difficult enough trying to function as it was, being constantly in the studio, travelling and having to go through customs all the time. Essentially, nobody wanted to get busted, although we were always worried about Glen carrying something. So we would have to go through his stuff first before the customs agents did.

I do remember one time back in Ohio when someone put some Angel Dust or PCP in some pot and we smoked it. We were on stage and suddenly Neal was playing this drum solo with a couple of dead fish! He took a snare roll and these fish scales start flying everywhere. All I remember was I was so high that my guitar neck just seemed like it went on for miles — it stretched way out — and whenever I went to play a chord my arm and the guitar neck were just miles away.

By the *School's Out* period we felt we really had our finger on the pulse of what the kids were into. For instance, the title song is still a teen anthem. I mean, going to school is the most common factor in juvenile life. And what moment of the school year does every kid look forward to? Summer — when school's out. And "school's out forever" is the ultimate dream to a kid.

That opening guitar riff to "School's Out" was written by Glen. Probably his most notable contribution. Although funnily enough, when *Guitar Player* magazine voted on the best guitar riffs of the past twenty years a couple of years back — Glen got in — not for "Schools Out" but for "I'm Eighteen". Anyway, I worked on the middle section with the piano — the "No more pencils, no more rules" bit. Originally only Alice and I got writing credits for that song. Somehow, Neal got BMI to add him, Dennis and Glen to the credits later — but that wasn't really the case at all.

"Gutter Cat vs The Jets" began with a bass riff that Dennis had been kicking around for a while. I really liked it and persuaded him to work it up. It had a very raga type feel at the beginning. We had this piano that we bought in Michigan and I learned the song on it and added some stuff. The *West Side Story* theme came later when we were in the studio with Bob.

"Blue Turk" came from a sort of a buzz word at the time — the Blue Turk Cafe, yeh daddy-o. The feel was very much influenced by Dennis' beatnik bass part. This was the only song I wrote by myself on *School's Out*.

"The Grand Finale" was Bob Ezrin's finishing touch, a little "Walk On The Wild Side" and a little "School's Out" vamp on the chorus section. That song was written to tie the whole album together — put a knot on it so to speak. Probably not what most hard-core Cooper fans were used to hearing from us. During the stage show we played this song to a backing tape which was kind of neat — first time we had ever done that.

"Alma Mater" was primarily written by Neal, especially the part which goes, "rain is falling down my cheek, searching for the sea." Again it had a kind of Beatles tinge to it which I think came off pretty well. But I wrote the part, "come on everybody, I hope that I will see you again". I don't want to sound egotistical but there really wasn't a song that we did that I didn't write something on.

In fact, on the *School's Out* album I was not credited for writing most of the songs, like I had been on the previous two records. I didn't even get a credit for "Looney Tune" which I should have. I wanted the rest of the band to share in it. Now that I come to think about it, not exactly the smartest move financially on my part. But this was my way of keeping the peace in the band at the time.

I really think in a lot of ways the songwriting credits were all wrong. I mean Dennis wrote a lot of stuff, yet some songs Dennis should have got credit he didn't and on some things he did get credit he shouldn't have, same with Alice. Glen never wrote a song — he wrote guitar parts, yet he got writing credits. I think the band really didn't understand what a songwriter got paid for. You get paid for the melody. You get mechanical royalties for parts and arrangements — but that shouldn't come out of the song publishing.

For the *School's Out* album cover Pacific Eye & Ear were involved. We obviously had a much larger budget from Warner Bros than we'd had for *Killer*. We came up with the idea for the desk and carved our names in it and Drew the artist at Pacific designed the fold-out desktop cover. They also came up with the panties idea — that was pure genius. When you pulled the record out of its outer sleeve, instead of being wrapped in the usual dust sleeve, it was wrapped in a pair of disposable paper panties.

School's Out was very different as a concept album — it was certainly very different to *Killer*. We were trying new things on stage and especially in the production end of things with Bob Ezrin. It was a good album, but not our best in my opinion. I think it was a bit overproduced with the horns and stuff. It was such a drastic leap from the hard edge of *Killer* that I'm sure a lot fans were turned off by it. It was a very Vaudeville type of record. Because of the stage show and sheer popularity of the track "School's Out", we had managed to outdo *Killer*, but I still think that song-wise *Killer* had the better material.

The album was released in July 1972 and got into the top 20. The "School's Out" single was a perfect summer song released in a summer lacking in good hits and became our biggest hit in the UK reaching number 1 — as a result that June we flew over and played one date at the Wembley Arena, supported by a then unknown band called Roxy Music.

In England, there were now apparently armies of outraged parents who wanted us banned from even entering their shores. Obviously the rumours about dismembered chickens and outrageous hanging stunts had preceded us. Despite these protests, our whole travelling glitz and kitsch extravaganza hit Wembley Arena — with not a chicken in sight I might add.

However, I do remember that we staged this great publicity stunt — I say "we", but I for one was not consulted. It was typical of the type of business decisions that were beginning to be taken that we were unaware of. On the side of this large truck was a billboard of the famous picture of Alice naked, with the snake wrapped around him, from the cover of *Rolling Stone* magazine. The day of the show, a driver was hired to stall the truck in downtown London during rush hour. The traffic was backed up for miles and it made all the news reports that evening — unbelievable publicity.

Alice's reputation as an evil incarnation had also been enhanced when, during the flight over to England, the old lady in the next seat to him passed away in her sleep. The press understandably had a field day. Alice later speculated that he should have drawn two vampire tooth marks on her neck for major effect. She was dead after all, it was hardly as if she was going to object.

We continued to tour through the US for the rest of the summer. Although we were playing in bigger and bigger arenas, critically the LP was not greeted with the same approval that had been heaped on *Killer*. Although *Rolling Stone* described it as an ambitious album, they qualified it by saying that it was "aimless musically as it is lyrically". At the end of the review Ben Gersen said he was waiting for David Bowie, who he termed "a more credible transvestite" to hit the States.

As we had never really wanted to be seen as transvestites, credible or otherwise, that didn't particularly bother us. I suppose it was in some ways inevitable that we would be lumped in with other acts that wore make-up or flashy clothes like David Bowie, Marc Bolan, Iggy Pop and Lou Reed. In England this was mainly termed the "glam rock" movement, which was spearheaded by people like Bowie and Bolan.

But we never really thought of ourselves as being a glam band like The Sweet or Slade. We considered ourselves much more of a hard rock band with a lot more psychedelic overtones. Now I look back on it, it was just something that was happening both in the United States and the UK. I remember seeing David Bowie at the Radio City Music Hall with the Spiders from Mars with Mick Ronson. Bowie came down suspended from the ceiling, it was pretty outrageous. It was like going to a play. It was a reasonable rock show, it was fun, it was trippy, it was something different. It was not like going to see Boston just standing there playing their guitars, not doing anything.

But we weren't really concerned with labels. We didn't really mind if the press lumped us in with the glam bands. I mean, any publicity was good publicity. I think in general we had a good relationship with the press. I think they liked us because there were a lot of interesting angles to write about. In *16 Magazine* I got an award for the best chest in rock and roll! So there was the cutesy thing, then there was the "Alice tell us all about the dark side" angle.

On the *School's Out* tour I remember the Hollywood Bowl show with Flo and Eddie being particularly memorable. Mo Osten's (head of Warner Bros) son came to see the show, he was a real butthead. He got himself into some fight which spilled over into our dressing room. I remember getting really pissed off and throwing the kid out.

Wolfman Jack came riding out on a camel to introduce us. Ringo was there

Above: Dennis Dunaway. *Photo: Torn Ticket Productions*

Above: Glen Buxton. *Photo: Torn Ticket Productions*

and Elton John. Because the *School's Out* LP came with a free pair of panties, we had a helicopter drop thousands of pairs of panties on the audience. There was a big thing in the newspapers about how Alice Cooper had these panties seized by customs agents because there was no fire retardent in them. It was a great bit of publicity. The headlines read, "Alice Cooper's panties seized by US Customs".

After the show I remember going to the Rainbow Club on Sunset Boulevard with Alice, Elton John and Ringo. Elton said to Alice, "Alice, you really showed me what show business is all about" and it wasn't long after that Elton started wearing big feather plumes and all his outrageous costumes. Also I think his song "All The Young Girls Love Alice" is sort of a tribute to the Alice Cooper group — anyway that's what Cindy Lang told me.

Queen were also big fans of ours. I remember this bass player friend I knew named Frank Crandell, who had married Alice's sister, came up to me one day and said, "Hey Mike, Queen are playing in Hartford, Connecticut — can you get us tickets?" I said, "Sure" and made a few calls and got some tickets to the show. Someone asked me if I'd like to meet the band and I said, "Sure, they put on a good show". I went backstage and all the guys in the band came up to me and said, "Wow — it's a real honour to meet you — we're really big fans." They were really gassed and I didn't even know much about them up until then. I remember talking to Brian May and he was telling me about making his own guitar.

A weird incident happened when we were out on the road on the *School's Out* tour. We were staying in Sacramento, and this girl came up to me and gave me this red sailor's jacket — it was from some play called *The Visit* apparently. Anyway, she also gave me this old single from the 1950's. On one side was a track called "School's Out" and on the other side was a song called "Alley Cat". I can't recall who the artist was, but we had never even seen or heard of them before. We thought this was really bizarre because our single had "School's Out" on the A side and "Gutter Cat" on the flip side. It was fucking strange to say the least.

The stage show for *School's Out* wasn't that different from the *Killer* tour. Essentially the gallows was such a good thing we weren't going to let it go just yet. So we carried on with our nightly hanging of Alice. But instead of doing it after the "Dead Babies" segment, we replaced it with a sequence based around "Gutter Cat". We would stage a mock street fight where Neal would jump over his drums and attack Alice. Then I would go at Alice with a knife and he'd hit me on the head with a fake wax bottle. Then he would flip me over onto this mat on the floor and it looked like he'd killed me. It looked very realistic. I had always wanted to be a stunt man when I was a kid.

Then the police sirens would wail and the next thing Alice has his hands tied behind his back and Glen has a torch and a hood on dressed as a priest and wheels him off to the gallows for killing me in this street crime. Then Neal would walk behind with the big snare drum playing the death dirge and lead him to the gallows. He fell through the trap door and hung there. It was great. We would have lightning and strobes going and then do a quick costume change and then we would go into this real light song, to provide that real contrast. Again the idea of a rebirth after the death sequence.

The *School's Out* tour, complete with gallows and all, went back to Europe in a blaze of publicity in November 1972. There was a near riot in Glasgow, and then it was Belgium, Sweden, Denmark, Holland, Germany and Switzerland. By this time we could afford those little touring extravagances. Hotel rooms were generally strewn with beer bottles, whiskey bottles, and more beer bottles. Certain band members had hired projectors to show old John Wayne movies, as the TV wasn't exactly to their liking. Then there was all the usual bad taste jokes and clowning around. It felt a bit like an American rock 'n' roll army on manoeuvres in Europe. Playing outside of America was real interesting, just to see what they made of our show. When we played in Belgium it was like Beatlemania. But virtually every place we went we got strange or different reactions. In Sweden everyone was so quiet, so we guessed we hadn't gone down too well and then at the end of the show they kind of exploded into applause.

Then, when we played the Olympia Theatre in Paris someone drove a Citroen car through the front door. The place only held about 1,500 people and it was completely sold out and some crazy French man got into his car and drove it through the front of the theatre. I remember Mick and Bianca Jagger were there with Charlie Watts. Alice was hanging out with his latest celebrity friend Omar Shariff. For some reason the band was really hip in France. It was odd as the French don't really seem to like the average American. But in our case they seemed to make an exception.

After the show I remember we were hanging out with Bianca Jagger and Pierre Cardin who was a big fan of ours. We went to this club and I remember

Neal was asking for Smirnoff Vodka. The barman told him that they hadn't got any. Anyway, Pierre Cardin hops into this taxi, goes back to his flat, and brings back a bottle of Smirnoff with him. We weren't really that fussy, but Neal was flattered nonetheless.

Above: Dennis Dunaway and Glen Buxton. *Photo: Torn Ticket Productions*

Billion Dollar Babies

After *School's Out* we moved full time from the farm in Pontiac, Michigan to the Galecie Estate in Greenwich, Connecticut. By this time we were making enough money to afford the extravagance of a band mansion. Connecticut was certainly rather an odd place for a band to be. So upper class, everything closed at ten o'clock. Very strange scene. Perhaps we would have been a lot better off living in New York City. But it was on our new estate that we started planning our next assault on the record industry. The single "School's Out" had been a worldwide hit and the band had truly arrived. Alice Cooper was a household name. As a result, no part of our image was now being left to chance.

However, by the time we had moved everything onto the estate, it was really clear that there were differences appearing about the way the group should be developing. Dennis for one was becoming more and more introverted as the band got further away from what his concept of the Alice Cooper group was. I think he still envisioned the group as being like the early Pink Floyd — a kind of a mind set. But increasingly Bob Ezrin had taken that kind of freakiness out of the band and made it slick. You have to remember Dennis was really into the avant-garde side of things. But having said that, the Dunaways were probably the most normal of all of us at the Connecticut estate.

At the estate, which had originally been built by some Broadway producer, we all pretty much had a floor of our own — after all there were about 40

CashBox Top 100 Albums

1 BILLION DOLLAR BABIES ALICE COOPER (Warner Bros. BS 2685)	34 SLOPPY SECONDS DR. HOOK & THE MEDICINE SHOW (Columbia KC 31789) (CT/CA 31789)	67 DOUG SAHM AND BAND (Atlantic SD 7254)
2 ROCKY MOUNTAIN HIGH JOHN DENVER (RCA LSP 4731) (P8S/PK 1972)	35 COSMIC WHEELS DONOVAN (Epic KE 32156)	68 SITTIN' IN LOGGINS & MESSINA (Columbia 31044)
3 THE DARK SIDE OF THE MOON PINK FLOYD (Harvest SMAS 11163) (Dist. Capitol)	36 BYRDS (Asylum SD 5054) (Dist. Atlantic)	69 CHUCK BERRY GOLDEN DECADE VOL. 2 (Chess CH 1514)
4 DUELLING BANJOS ERIC WEISSBERG, STEVE MANDEL, "N" MARSHALL BRICKMAN (Warner Bros. BS 2683)	37 LOST HORIZON ORIGINAL SOUNDTRACK (Bell 1300)	70 SKYWRITER JACKSON FIVE (Motown M761L)
5 LADY SINGS THE BLUES DIANA ROSS/SOUNDTRACK (Motown M 758 D)	38 LAST DAYS & TIME EARTH, WIND & FIRE (Columbia 31622) (CT/CA 31622)	71 HOMECOMING AMERICA (Warner Bros. BS 2655) (M8/M5 2655)
6 DON'T SHOOT ME I'M ONLY THE PIANO PLAYER ELTON JOHN (MCA 2100)	39 BLACK CAESAR JAMES BROWN, ORIGINAL SOUNDTRACK (Polydor PD 6014)	72 GREEN IS BLUE AL GREEN (Hi 6065, 32095) (Dist. London)
7 SHOOT OUT AT THE FANTASY FACTORY TRAFFIC (Island SW 9323) (Dist. Capitol)	40 I'M STILL IN LOVE WITH YOU AL GREEN (Hi 7169, 32074) (Dist. London)	73 PLEASURE OHIO PLAYERS (Westbound R2017) (Dist. Chess)
8 MASTERPIECE TEMPTATIONS (Gordy G 965L) (Dist. Motown)	41 THE SESSION JERRY LEE LEWIS (Mercury SRM 2-803)	74 ROUND 2 STYLISTICS (Avco AV 11006)
9 ELVIS ALOHA FROM HAWAII VIA SATELLITE ELVIS PRESLEY (RCA VPSX 6089) (P8S/PK 6144)	42 BEGINNINGS ALLMAN BROTHERS BAND (Atco SD 2-805) (Dist. Atlantic)	75 THE BEST OF B. B. KING (ABC ABCX-767)
10 THEY ONLY COME AT NIGHT EDGAR WINTER (Epic KE 31584)	43 ACROSS 110TH STREET BOBBY WOMACK & PEACE, J. J. JOHNSON, ORIGINAL MOTION PICTURE SCORE (United Artists UAS 5225)	76 LOUDON WAINWRIGHT III (Columbia KC 31462)
11 CAN'T BUY A THRILL STEELY DAN (ABC ABCX 758) (8/5 758)	44 HEARTBREAKER FREE (Island SW 9324) (Dist. Capitol)	77 TOMMY LONDON SYMPHONY ORCHESTRA & CHAMBER CHOIR WITH GUEST SOLOISTS (Ode SP 99001) (Dist. A&M)
12 NO SECRETS CARLY SIMON (Elektra EKS 75049)	45 GRAND HOTEL PROCOL HARUM (Chrysalis CHR 1037) (Dist. W.B.)	78 CATCH BULL AT FOUR CAT STEVENS (A&M SP 4365) (8T/CS 4365)
13 PRELUDE DEODATO (CTI 6021)	46 COMPOSITE TRUTH MANDRILL (Polydor PD 5043)	79 HURRICANE SMITH (Capitol ST 11099)
14 WATTSTAX VARIOUS ARTISTS (Stax STS-2-3010) (Dist. Columbia)	47 SLAYED? SLADE (Polydor PD 5524)	80 THE 2nd CRUSADE CRUSADERS (Blue Thumb BTS 7000) (Famous)
15 BIRDS OF FIRE MAHAVISHNU ORCHESTRA (Columbia KC 31996)	48 AMERICA, WHY I LOVE HER JOHN WAYNE (RCA LSP 4828) (P8S/PK 2122)	81 TROUBLE MAN MARVIN GAYE, ORIGINAL MOTION PICTURE SOUNDTRACK (Tamla T329L) (Dist. Motown)
16 THE WORLD IS A GHETTO WAR (United Artists UAS 5652)	49 EDWARD BEAR (Capitol 11157)	82 SUMMER BREEZE SEALS & CROFTS (Warner Bros. BS 2629) (M8/M5 2629)
17 SPACE ODDITY DAVID BOWIE (RCA LSP 4813) (P8S/PK 2265)	50 LIFE & TIMES JIM CROCE (ABC ABCX 769)	83 THE FIRST SONGS LAURA NYRO (Columbia KE 31410)
18 THE DIVINE MISS M BETTE MIDLER (Atlantic SD 7238) (TP/CA 7238)	51 THE CAPTAIN AND ME DOOBIE BROTHERS (Warner Bros. BS 2694)	84 RHYMES & REASONS CAROLE KING (Ode SP 77016) (8T/CS 77016) (Dist. A&M)
19 MOVING WAVES FOCUS (Sire SAS-7401) (Dist. Paramount)	52 THE BEST OF THE JAMES GANG FEATURING JOE WALSH (ABC ABCX-774)	85 CREEDENCE GOLD CREEDENCE CLEARWATER (Fantasy 9413)
20 TALKING BOOK STEVIE WONDER (Tamla 319) (Dist. Motown)	53 THE BEST OF MOUNTAIN (Columbia KC 31678)	86 A LETTER TO MYSELF CHI-LITES (Brunswick 754188)
21 THE BEST OF BREAD (Elektra EKS 75056)	54 ALONE TOGETHER DONNY OSMOND (MGM SE 4886)	87 WILL THE CIRCLE BE UNBROKEN NITTY GRITTY DIRT BAND (United Artists 9801)
22 NEITHER ONE OF US GLADYS KNIGHT & THE PIPS (Soul 737) (Dist. Motown)	55 IN CONCERT DEREK & THE DOMINOS (RSO-2-8800) (Dist. Atlantic)	88 CHAPTER VII BUDDY MILES BAND (Columbia KC 32204)
23 TRUE STORIES AND OTHER DREAMS JUDY COLLINS (Elektra 75053)	56 1962-1966 THE BEATLES (Apple SKBO 3403) (Dist. Capitol)	89 MY SECOND ALBUM DONNA FARGO (Dot DOS 26000) (Dist. Famous)
24 WHO DO WE THINK WE ARE? DEEP PURPLE (Warner Bros. 2678)	57 1967-1970 THE BEATLES (Apple SKBO 3404) (Dist. Capitol)	90 16 GREATEST HITS STEPPENWOLF (Dunhill DSX 50135)
25 EAT IT HUMBLE PIE (A&M SP 3701)	58 HOUSE OF THE HOLY LED ZEPPELIN (Atlantic SD 7255)	91 LIVING TOGETHER GROWING TOGETHER 5th DIMENSION (Bell 1116)
26 AROUND THE WORLD WITH THREE DOG NIGHT (Dunhill DTS 50138)	59 ME & MRS. JONES JOHNNY MATHIS (Columbia KC 32114)	92 CYMANDE (Janus JLS 3044)
27 KEEPER OF THE CASTLE FOUR TOPS (Dunhill DS 50129)	60 DOUBLE GOLD NEIL DIAMOND (Bang B502-227)	93 GODSPELL ORIGINAL CAST (Bell 1102) (8/5 1102)
28 TRANSFORMER LOU REED (RCA LSP 4807) (P8S/PK 2665)	61 STEALERS WHEEL (A&M SP 4377)	94 RAUNCH N' ROLL LIVE BLACK OAK ARKANSAS (Atco SD 7019) (Dist. Atlantic)
29 I AM WOMAN HELEN REDDY (Capitol ST 11068)	62 TAPESTRY CAROLE KING (Ode SP 77009)	95 CLAPTON ERIC CLAPTON (Polydor PD 5526)
30 LOGGINS & MESSINA (Columbia KC 31748) (CT/CA 31748)	63 BIRTH DAY NEW BIRTH (RCA LSP 4797) (P8S/PK 2079)	96 THE POWER OF JOE SIMON (Spring SPR 5704) (Dist. Polydor)
31 SEVENTH SOJOURN MOODY BLUES (Threshold THS 7) (Dist. London)	64 BECK, BOGART & APPICE (Epic KE 32140)	97 BITE DOWN HARD 30 JO BONNE (Asylum SD 5065) (Dist. Atlantic)
32 HOT AUGUST NIGHT NEIL DIAMOND (MCA 20000)	65 THE SINGER LIZA MINNELLI (Columbia KC 32149)	98 SUPER FLY CURTIS MAYFIELD—Original Motion Picture, Soundtrack (Curtom CRS 8014)
33 HOLLAND BEACH BOYS (Brother/Reprise MS 2118)	66 FOR THE ROSES JONI MITCHELL (Asylum SD 5057) (CT/CA 5057) (Dist. Atlantic)	99 360° OF BILLY PAUL (Phila. Int'l 31793) (Dist. Columbia)
		100 LIVING IN THE PAST JETHRO TULL (Chrysalis 2CH 1035) (M8/M5 1035) (Dist. W.B.)

rooms in total. Each guy was responsible for his own space. We had house-keepers who would come in and clean up. Neal and I were on the top floor, we had two rooms each, Charlie, our lighting engineer, lived in a room off the top floor, in a kind of closet. He was really getting into the occult. I think he was doing all kinds of weird things in there. Glen was on the next floor. He had cut a hole in the wall so he could show his movies. Then Alice had the big room downstairs with the four sided shower room with 16 nozzles, shower heads coming at you from all directions.

The Galecie Estate was huge. It even had servants' quarters out the back where the roadies lived. There was a large rehearsal room, even a ballroom that could hold twelve hundred people. The ballroom had big glass windows all along the sides and a false wall for the orchestra which opened at the top so you could hear the music without seeing the players. We hung a dummy from the ceiling. That's where we did all the rehearsals and pre-productions for the album which became *Billion Dollar Babies*. Bob Ezrin then brought the remote recording unit from the Record Plant to the estate — he oversaw the recordings with Jack Douglas who went on to work with Cheap Trick, Aerosmith and John Lennon.

By this time we were making good money and our company Alice Cooper Incorporated was doing really well. When we were touring we were each making around $35,000 a year. Then there was the mechanicals (album sales) and the publishing money which came next. I remember going to New York to get my first publishing check for $90,000 for the *Billion Dollar Babies* album. For the first time since leaving Phoenix I went out and bought a car. I got a Jaguar and Neal got a couple of Rolls Royces, Dennis got a T-bird. Alice, as I remember, couldn't drive at the time.

At the estate all our rent and food and other expenditure were paid for. But now we all had money, it was really the beginning of the end. It was ironic but as soon as we started to make some serious money we got to the point where we didn't want to live together any more.

One of the problems was that Alice and I were writing most of the mate-rial, hence we were making more than the rest of the band. So if we each made $100,000 in six months then Neal, Dennis, and Glen probably only got $30,000 — you can imagine how that went down. I don't know if those guys felt that their songs were getting passed over or they weren't being treated fairly or what. I pushed hard for my songs and so did Dennis. The bottom line always depended on whether the song would work well in the show or the album concept. A lot of the final choice was down to Bob Ezrin and Shep. They would get together and listen to our songs and had a definite input on what would get released. My songs just seemed to be more catchy and more musical.

All the basic tracks for the *Billion Dollar Babies* album were recorded at the estate in Connecticut except for "Hello Hooray" and "Generation Landslide". I remember one particularly weird incedent happening one Halloween night when we were recording. There was a knock at the front door. When we opened it there was a grave stone leaning up against the door. On the stone was the name of two infants that had died. Some sick person had obviously dug it up and left it on our door step. We called the police and they came and picked it up — it was really bizarre.

After the bed tracks were completed, we went to the Record Plant in New York to do some overdubs. While we were there, Yes were also recording. I hung out with Chris Squire for a while. He was a really nice guy. I remember him being a big fan of Dennis's bass style. He thought Dennis was great. I also remember talking to him once at the Ashes Club. He said to me that he thought Dennis never got the credit he deserved. Mind you, I don't think any of us got the credit we deserved!

We finished the *Billion Dollar Babies* album at Morgan Studios in England. I enjoyed the different production elements; recording the basic tracks at the estate then doing overdubs at the studio in New York and then finishing the album off in England. It was almost like The Beatles or something. Truly a continental style to it. It felt like we had really come into our own.

But I was less impressed with the sessions in England with the supposed "celebrity line-up" including Marc Bolan and Harry Nilsson — rock 'n' roll bums hanging out and getting drunk. A lot of times it wasn't very pleasant being at the studio with these so-called "stars", unless you were incredibly rude and obnoxious because that was what you had to do to stay in the forefront with these people.

I remember a lot of egos flying during that time. I think Harry Nilsson was a real asshole. At the recording session he was stinking drunk. Well Nilsson started giving me a bunch of shit for no reason at all. Finally I stood up and picked up the table we were sitting around and I was ready to throw it at him. Our road manager grabbed me and held my arms. Donovan was there as well.

He was really nice — he was just a very sensitive guy sitting there with his guitar. I remember Keith Moon being there also.

Alice and Neal liked to play a lot of pool. Back home at our mansion they had this ongoing competition while the rest of us used to tune up — in fact I think Alice still owes Neal $65. So, while we were in London we're hanging out with Elton John, Bernie Taupin, Ronnie Lane and Ronnie Wood. We're round at one of their houses and there's a snooker table there. So Alice and Neal figure they're so shit hot at pool they could beat everyone at snooker — after all it had a cue stick, balls and a baize table. Naturally, they got their butts kicked a couple of times, but they eventually ended up winning a game.

I think the idea was that having these people hanging around would also be great publicity for the album, even though I don't hear Bolan or Nilsson on any of the tracks. There were a number of jam sessions, but they didn't make it onto the album. But Alice would say these people were on there — it was good publicity for the band. But personally I think it just made us look cheap. Donovan was on the album. I remember when we were down at Morgan Studios, he was hanging around the studio at that moment so that's how he wound up singing on the title track. Originally Alice sang "we go nightly in the attic...." on the first chorus, and Donovan sang it on the second one. And then I said, "Hey, Alice needs to be on both parts. Lets do a sort of 'row, row your boat type thing' where Alice sings the first chorus while Donovan speaks it and Donovan sings the second chorus while Alice speaks it". To my surprise Bob Ezrin said, "Great idea, let's do it" It was getting to the point where I was amazed when they listened to any of my ideas.

The title *Billion Dollar Babies* came from some Hollywood magazine we picked up that had these starlet pin-ups with the headline "billion dollar babies" — that sounded good, why change it? The song itself evolved from a jam session I had with this friend of Glen's called Rocking Reggie Vincent. I'd be playing piano and Glen wouldn't show up for rehearsals, so Reggie would bring his guitar and we'd start jamming. Reggie was from Detroit (he's now a minister out in Phoenix). He was always hanging out with us in early '73. Reggie was alright — but kind of a pain in the ass. He was always around, anytime we'd get together he was there. Anyway he was doing what Glen should have been doing. Eventually Glen would show up two and a half hours later when we were ready to quit.

"Unfinished Sweet" was written with the show in mind — the idea was to make it a musical trip to the dentist. In the show Alice would attack this big tooth with a giant toothbrush and at the end brush it. Also we used the giant drill in this part of the show. The idea of a dancing tooth came from an old TV commercial of a dancing pack of Chesterfield cigarettes. Cindy Smith was the dancer in the show, dressed as the giant tooth with her legs sticking out the bottom. It was another song that had a James Bond-ish middle section to it that I really liked.

Alice got together with Bob Ezrin and they wrote "I Love The Dead". Alice had gotten Dick Wagner to come in and help with some of the guitar lines. To be honest I would have never written a song like that, because it was such a dark piece of music. I wrote the chorus section to lighten it up a bit.

"No More Mr Nice Guy" was actually a song I had been kicking around since the *Killer* days which we had never gotten around to recording. But I jammed on it all the time — typically everyone had heard most of my songs because I'd play them during tune-ups and rehearsals. The guys would say, "Hey let's use that..." It was typical of a song where I would have a verse and chorus and Alice would come up with a line or two. Same with the other guys. I was always famous for writing the first verse and chorus and then not being able to come up with something for the second verse. In the end Alice and I were credited as writing the original lyrics and we split the publishing 50/50, even though in reality I wrote most of the song.

For "Elected" the story goes that Alice sang his vocal in the studio looking into a full length mirror. Apparently the idea was that he should try and sell himself the idea of getting elected. Well I never heard about that until the *Prime Cuts* video came out, so I don't know if that's true or not. By this time Alice was increasingly becoming "the star" and preferred to sing alone in the studio. It was typical of the way that they were separating the band from Alice — it was something I feel Shep and Bob had a lot to do with. "Elected" originally came from a song called "Reflected" off the *Pretties For You* album. We changed it and put it on *Billion Dollar Babies*.

I remember when we had finished at Morgan Studios we needed one more song for the record and everybody was kind of sick of the weather in England which was crummy. So the whole band with David Leibert (our road manager) went down to the Canary Islands. We were looking for a place where we could rehearse and write. What they found was this half-finished luxury hotel.

Above: Michael Bruce. *Photo: Torn Ticket Productions*

So we checked in — there was nobody there but us and the people working on the building. We all thought this was great until 5.30 the next morning when, "bang, bang bang", the construction workers started pounding nails and everything. This went on every fucking morning except weekends. But I guess we would get so drunk we eventually slept through it.

We set up all our gear in the top penthouse, and that's where we wrote the last song for the album — "Generation Landslide". Glen came up with some licks for that song and Alice played harp, it was great. It was like we had temporarily reverted to being a cohesive band. The group had this amazing ability to pop back if we were just given some time to ourselves. It just showed that once left alone, without every genius in the world trying to figure out what was good for us, we could do just fine.

But Shep and Bob Ezrin were really starting to steer the direction of the band towards the Broadway idea. In my opinion it was the wrong direction. That Broadway thing was part of the band, but definitely not the whole thing. They thought they knew what the kids wanted. Well, in my opinion, what the kids wanted was the raunchy hard-edged Alice, not the Broadway stuff. I think the decision to move in this direction was what really helped to kill the band off.

I really felt that "No More Mr Nice Guy" should have been the first single to be taken off the *Billion Dollar Babies* album, but I think that idea was rejected because it wasn't in keeping with the theme of the record. Instead "Hello Hooray" ended up being the first single — it was also an obvious choice for the opening song of the stage show. Again it was more in keeping with Shep and Alice's interpretation of that top hat and cane thing. Oddly, on the single version, the slide guitar solo in the middle was cut out — another decision I wasn't informed about. Eventually, "No More Mr Nice Guy" did get released as a single and it was our biggest hit in the States. I even received a BMI certificate of achievement for it.

"Elected" turned out to be the second single. We did our first video for that song, although again I say "we" but most of it was filmed in New York with only Alice. Again, something we weren't consulted about. The video clip mostly follows Alice around on a mock presidential campaign. The whole idea of the character of Alice Cooper, one of the most notorious figures in rock, standing for President was a surreal enough notion for anyone. Emerging from stretched limos to press flesh and greet the public, Alice is in his pink top hat and tails, leering at the prospective voters. The video ends in chaos with Alice in his election office, complete with a cigarette smoking chimpanzee as his campaign manager. Drowning in dollar bills and telephone cables, he finally sinks into his chair in submission.

I remember we were out on the road when the album finally came out in February 1973. I listened to it in my hotel room and just got this really big smile. I was thinking, "It's amazing, we're really pulling this off". The album was very, very unique and very, very different. I was really proud of the songs, especially "No More Mr. Nice Guy", "Billion Dollar Babies" and "Generation Landslide". I kind of had mixed feelings about "I Love The Dead" — it wasn't my personal taste — but I understood the importance of that macabre thing to the album. That was the great thing about having five individuals in the band, you didn't always just focus on Alice. The different styles really showed through in the music.

The *Billion Dollar Babies* tour was our biggest ever. We played seventy-plus cities in three months. With *Billion Dollar Babies* a number 1 album on both sides of the Atlantic, no expense was spared. The tour started in Rochester, New York on March 5th, and such was our upward trajectory, by the time we reached Madison Square Garden three months later we had played to 800,000 people who had paid over $4.5 million for the privilege. The press were flown from New York to Philadelphia for the tour launch and supplied with champagne all the way.

Our touring party, which included support band Flo and Eddie, all travelled in a Boeing 707 jet named "The Starship" which had Alice Cooper and a black dollar sign painted on the side. In no time at all, the plane was a scene of touring mayhem. It was also used by Led Zeppelin, The Stones, Jefferson Starship and others. Graffiti adorned the walls, loud rock 'n' roll blared from the speakers, spent beer cans littered the aisles. There was a lot of wildness going on. There was a bedroom and a bathroom and everyone wanted to try it out and to see what it was like to have a girl at 30,000 feet. It was outrageous. They tore out all the seats to the plane, they had videos and a bar.

Joe Gannon was hired to design the stage set which in itself cost $150,000. The stage had all these boxes built on top of each other in which the band members played, it was as if we were all appearing in a weird rock 'n roll version of Hollywood Squares. For the finale, the US flag was rolled out while a tape of Kate Smith singing "God Bless America" blared out of the speakers.

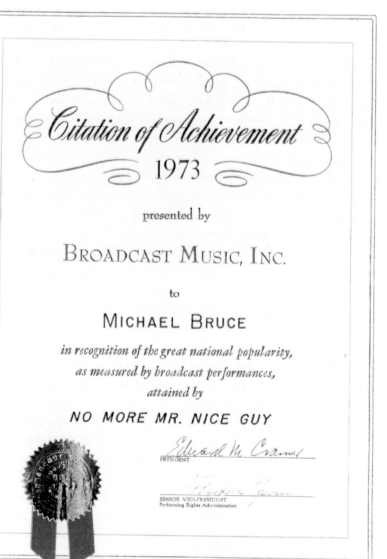

The hanging sequence had now been replaced by a guillotining.

Amazing Randi, the magician, came up with the guillotine. It was from an old vaudeville act that hadn't been used since the 1920's. In the end Amazing Randi played the executioner on stage. Anyway the guillotine illusion was very real — the only way you could tell it was a fake was if you used a camera. We thought that was great. So Warner Bros built us this guillotine and I remember when we first got it Alice wouldn't stick his head in it. Everybody tried it except Alice. Finally one night he got really drunk and did it. It was pretty scary because it was a real metal blade. The blade wasn't real sharp but falling at that speed it didn't have to be. It still would have cut your head off.

The guillotine was very interesting in how it worked. Along the runners of the side of the head of the blade were long metal rods that ran down and tripped the bottom of the stock that held Alice's head in place. That flipped up and his head went down. Then the blade came down and another stock behind it would spring right into its place. So it looked like the original stock never disappeared. Then Amazing Randi would reach in the basket and pull out Alice's fake head — with the blood and everything — it really worked great.

At that time there were very few other rock 'n' roll acts that were trying to stage such an elaborate show on the scale we were. We were really the forerunners in that respect. We were forever wanting to do some more pyro stuff, but the fire marshals were always down there hassling us. The industry wasn't as slick as it is now. Nowadays, bands have gotten a lot more used to staging these kinds of things.

Even though the tour was actually our biggest and most successful, in reality it wasn't fun a lot of the time. Everything had gotten so big, it was in danger of spiralling out of control. The communication between the band and the management, and even between the individual band members, was breaking down. As a result, we were all getting increasingly unhappy — nobody liked the way things were being run. Soon Alice was the only one who knew the inside details — "If you have questions, ask Alice..." The *Billion Dollar Babies* stage was typical of what was going on.

"Here's what we've built — here's your new stage — like it?"

"What if we don't like it?"

"Too bad... You've already paid for it. You'll get used to it."

In fact they had covered the whole stage with pieces of metal flaked with glitter, which wasn't such a wonderful idea! When you brushed by something on the set you would either rip your clothes or cut your skin. Also they put poles in all the wrong spots. I remember bitching about it. Finally, three quarters of the way through the tour they relented and redesigned the stage, which could have been done in the first place if anybody had bothered to ask us. So they took out a couple of poles and in the process made me feel like a jerk for asking. Yet it was our fucking stage — we had paid for it. Again it was a case of us being told "we know what's best for the band".

So there was this growing unrest amongst the band — things just weren't right, the camaraderie was disappearing. Almost everything was being done without our knowledge or consent. There was no compassion between band and management. Most of the time we would react unfavourably to a good suggestion, because the decision was already made for us, and yet there was nothing we could do about it. We started to feel like, "Whose band is this anyway?"

During the *Babies* tour, Bob Greene did the interviews for his book *Billion Dollar Babies*. Basically, the band were at each others throats. When anyone would go back and talk with Bob Greene they would dish all the dirt they could on the rest of the guys — it was really pathetic. Again, I blame it on bad decisions. To me a manager is there to help the band make the decisions and give them some guidance, but not to do it for them and tell them how to run things. After all it was our band, at least it had been in the beginning.

In Bob Greene's book he equated the situation to something right out of Shakespeare, "Et tu Brute", and all that betrayal stuff. Well, it hadn't always

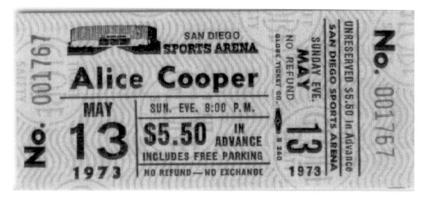

been like that. By the way, I've got to correct something in that book — there's a story where I'm going over to Frank Zappa's house to visit Pamela Zuberick (the original Suzie Creamcheese) over on Woodrow Wilson Drive in LA. I took the band vehicle and parked it in front of her house which is on a steep incline. So I'm walking away from the van and it started down the hill backwards. I ran as fast as I could to catch it as it was rolling toward Zappa's car. I made it to the van door and dived in — hit my knee on the asphalt and ripped my pants and bloodied my knee. I then jammed on the brakes with my hand and stopped the van inches away from Zappa's new Tornado. In the book, Bob wrote Alice into the story. Well folks, I was the only one there.

By the *Billion Dollar Babies* tour we were all drinking pretty heavily, except Dennis, who only drank a bit of wine. I think most of the time we drank to sedate ourselves, it was mainly the pressure of being on the road, the constant touring. But I think Alice's alcoholism started during the last period of the band. It got to the stage where Dennis and Neal didn't like driving with him. He got into a couple of near fatal wrecks. I think the problem was that there were people who would encourage Alice to drink heavily so he would get more outrageous on stage. As a result Alice was pretty sauced on every show towards the end. But most of the time he was in control, it was really Glen's drinking that was becoming the major problem.

In any event, Alice really wasn't a macho guy and neither was I — neither of us smoked cigarettes. He kept himself to himself a lot. He was real low key with the women probably so Cindy (Lang, his girlfriend) wouldn't find out. Alice used to play a bit of cards and gamble during the tours, but again for the most part he was pretty quiet. I think he didn't want people to think he was accessible, so he could keep up the mysterious image about himself.

At first I hadn't minded him being the star figure but when management tried to steer things away from the original concept of the band and started separating us from Alice, it began to bug me. Anyway, I was always too busy to be involved in the publicity aspects of the group like Alice was. For my part, if I wasn't down at the concert hall checking on the gear, I was out taking photos. I used to rent a car if we were in a city for a couple of days. I would go antique hunting, or looking for guitars.

All of us in the band were very likable really — even Glen — very personable. Despite what people thought, we weren't on huge ego trips. Alice was just a typical Aquarian, he loved the publicity angle. I think after being out on the road staying in one Holiday Inn after another, it was relief when we finally got to a town like New York, LA or Chicago. He would get the chance to go to some parties and meet these famous people. At the time I kind of resented Alice for all his name-dropping. I remember Alice doing these interviews and he would be constantly be mentioning people like George Burns, or Barry Goldwater, etc. Often we would be making faces and laughing behind his back while he was speaking because we thought he was talking bullshit.

But now I think it was perfectly natural. After all he was the centre of a lot of the attention, a focus. He wasn't a musician, he didn't play an instrument, so it was different kind of thing for him. He was a showman and the frontman of our band. Plus it was good publicity for us. Our publicist would arrange for photo opportunities with celebrities like George Burns, or Groucho Marx to have their photos taken or make news appearances with Alice.

I remember one publicity stunt, during Burns' Philharmonic Hall appearance, when Alice presented him with the "Alice Cooper Living Legend" award. The presentation with Burns and Jack Benny in attendance made for good copy. Barry Goldwater's name would come up from time to time due to the fact that Alice had bought the house next to Goldwater in Phoenix, which he had rented out to the president of a chemical corporation. Alice boasted. "The cool thing is, my house is bigger than his!"

Another of Alice's celebrity connections was the arch-surrealist painter Salvador Dali who had taken a shine to the idea of our band. With Dali's love of anything kitsch or over-the-top, he was no doubt amused by Alice's increasingly bizarre stunts and love for celebrity. The end result was that Alice and Dali struck up a friendship of sorts which seemed to be based mostly on confusion. I remember Alice saying something like, "Dali speaks in five different languages at once, and you're supposed to understand what he's talking about! We just stand there and then I'll say something that has nothing to do with what he's talking about. And then he'll say something back that has nothing to do with what I was talking about. We just go on like that".

I never got to meet Dali, or go to the unveiling of the artist's hologram of Alice at Knoedler Gallery in New York. I think I was out of town at the time. The piece itself was a picture of Alice together with a human brain and one of Dali's soft watches. Dali's pronouncement on the whole piece was that he had produced "a perfect reproduction of the brain of The Alice Cooperpopstar". I do remember we all had to pay $500 to build the thing. I guess it must still be

Above: Alice on stage in Rochester, New York. *Photo: Phillip Hendrix.*

stored in some warehouse somewhere. I'd love to see it now. But we invested in quite a few projects at the time. We gave some money to finance Stacey Keach's first movie *Busted*, he was a bit of a fan, he came to a couple of the shows.

Of course, as well as the attentions of celebrities, we also got a fair amount of attention from the opposite sex. But contrary to popular belief we didn't get a lot of groupies. Dennis was with Cindy Smith, so nothing there. Neal was with Babette. Glen was with pretty ordinary girls usually. He didn't get a lot of raving beauties — but hey, Glen had chicken bones hanging off of him so how attractive could he be, or smell for that matter. Alice was still with Cindy Lang, who he had first met when we were in Detroit in early 1971. She was a real smart girl, a real good-looker, thin and elf-like with real big eyes. As well as coming up with the title "Halo Of Flies", I think she helped Alice with lyrics and getting his stage look and act together. She was a real gutsy babe, and very much into his career. They were always together — inseparable. She had lived with him off and on from the days at the farm in Detroit.

So in an odd sort of way I guess I was the stud of the band. But I wasn't much of an exhibitionist, although I guess I had my share. I did have the two girls at once trip — the first time it was really enjoyable and the other time it was kind of uncomfortable because one of them was much more attractive than the other.

I guess some people will remember the song "We're An American Band" by Grand Funk Railroad with the line about "Sweet, sweet Connie". Well we had heard of her and got one of her cards — "See sweet Connie when you're in town". We were wondering about this chick. So we get to this town and we're staying at this two-storey Holiday Inn. There's this girl hanging around there and it's Connie. I had already heard the wild stories about her. So I grabbed her and took her to the hotel room to have sex because I wanted to be the first. I asked her, "What is it you like about bands so much?" And she goes, "They have power". She thought that because of all the attention and money that bands had power — go figure that one.

Later, I went to Shep's room and there she was dancing naked on the top of the table. Someone's got the video camera on. I think Glen was in there and David Leibert, our road manager. They asked me if I wanted to come in and I said "No", because I didn't feel like performing for everyone, if you know what I mean. I really wasn't into that. In the end I think she fucked everyone in the band and the road crew — she was one horny girl.

Then there was the time when I met this girl in Colorado. We were playing two nights at the Denver Coliseum. On the first night there was this girl who was sitting in the front row and she was real cute. We locked eyes all through the show and we met afterwards. It turned out she had a hotel room which her mom had gotten her. Well I didn't know this. I thought, "If she's got her own hotel room she must be old enough". She looked like she was over 18. So she spent the whole night with me.

Somehow her mother's boyfriend got all upset about this and told the girl's mother that I was going to take her on the road with me — which wasn't true. So before the next show a bunch of cops walk in and this chick was standing next to me. So the police ask, "Is this girl with anyone?" And I spoke up and said, "Yeh, she's with me". Well, our road manager then shouted, "No she's not..." I thought that was real weird — I didn't realize what was going on.

We go on stage and do the whole show. I come back off stage to change for the end of the show where we did the "God Bless America" bit with the Nixon impersonator, and sparklers etc. There's a taxi cab out back and my friend John Lewis, who came out from Arizona to see the show, says to me, "Michael get in the cab — we're going..." I said "What?" So I jump into the cab and all my stuff from the hotel room is in it. They told me that the police were backstage in the dressing room waiting to arrest me, and I had to get out of town. Well, later I found out about the whole misunderstanding and apologized to the girl's mother.

But these were isolated incidents. Much of that wild Alice Cooper group image was really a manufactured one. We were really just normal guys. But I guess when you are in the limelight a lot of people will tend to let their imaginations run wild about you. Neal was perhaps the wildest of the bunch. Neal liked to boast to Keith Moon that he had more drums than him. On occasions he could also match Moon's on tour antics.

I remember on one tour Neal got shit-faced drunk with one of our roadies, whose name was Goose. First they totally destroyed the hotel room they were in. Threw the TV out the window and stood the bed up on its end and ripped up all the sheets — tore the room apart. Then they went out into the hallway and took all the food trays and scattered them everywhere. Smeared food all over the walls. This guy Goose was a real nut and Neal was so drunk. Every time Goose would do something Neal had to outdo him. So finally they went over to the coke machine, Goose was a really big guy, so they walked the drinks machine to the stairwell and pushed it down the stairs. I heard this loud fucking noise. So I went into the hall to see what it was and Neal and Goose were laughing their asses off. I said, "Good job guys". I think Neal had to pay two or three thousand dollars for damages. Everybody really liked Neal.

I remember when Neal met Babette, his first wife. We were on the road at some hotel and he came to my room and said, "Hey man, there's a real Mike Bruce chick out here". And I go, "What do you mean?" And Neal says, "I really think she's your type".

So I went outside and checked her out. She was no less than 6'5" tall and I said, "Hey Neal, I think she's perfect for you" — maybe he was just trying to find out if I was interested in her. She had just moved down from Toronto. I remember him taking photos with her in furs sitting on the front of his limo — Neal's dream. Eventually Babette and Neal got married.

The *Billion Dollar Babies* tour ended up grossing a lot of money — something over $4 million. The only problem was that the expenses (which by that time included a beer tab of nine cases a day) totalled $3.5 million.

I think it was around that time we were supposed to be going to Japan. But we never made it. Alice and Shep flew over there and they were suffering from jet lag and annoyed the Japanese promoter over there. Apparently, it is considered rude if you don't eat the business meal. They didn't want to eat it because they were feeling sick, so the Japanese were insulted. And we didn't play in Australia either, two big disappointments.

Muscle Of Love

As the *Billion Dollar Babies* tour started winding down, we began flying home to Connecticut between some of the shows, especially if we were playing gigs like the Peachtree Pop Festival in Atlanta. We finished the main tour and then some extra shows were added — the Hollywood Bowl and others. Unfortunately we hadn't reserved the plane for long enough and Led Zeppelin took the "Starship" on tour. So the last dates had to be done without it.

As a result, when we played Arizona and we flew all of our parents out to see us play in Tucson, we had to hire this turbo prop plane — hell of a bumpy flight because they were flying over the desert in the summer. Another time we were at the Westchester Airport and it was the first time we'd flown in a Lear jet, I remember it because the pilot used to be Winston Churchill's personal pilot. And from there we got on a helicopter to the hotel. It was a real rock star type trip, playing the gig and then back on the helicopter to the hotel again.

Not only was the tour becoming a series of disjointed dates, but the band was fragmenting. Keeping the whole thing together was taking a large effort on everyone's part. For a start, Glen's drinking was becoming a major problem. It was Glen who really caused a lot of things to turn sour. Certainly, it really changed Alice's attitude toward the band. Glen was such a distraction, he would always leave lighted cigarette butts burning on the table. He made me nervous — I could not be around him for very long. Either he'd burn me with a cigarette, or some godawful thing would happen. It got to the point where I couldn't stay in the same room with him because I'd get asphyxiated with his chain smoking.

In the past Glen had been a very creative guitar player, but his timing was never especially good. He had always come up with a lot of his own guitar parts like the "School's Out" opening riff and the solo in "Dwight Frye", but a lot of times Bob Ezrin would really have to sit down with him to get something musical out of him. He would do all those bending guitar lines, Glen played a real good slide guitar and he was also a mean spoons player!

Early on, it had worked pretty well between Glen and me because as guitar players we were at totally different ends of the spectrum. I was more orthodox, I kind of played the straight-laced stuff because I came out of The Beatles genre. After all, my first band did Beatles and Beach Boys harmonies — that's what I liked. I had to pretty much play the straight rhythm and hold the fort so to speak because Dennis was all over the place as a bass guitar player. He tended to play a lot of notes in a busy style — which was distinct and interesting, but not exactly predictable. What with Neal also playing in a very loose style, they were a pretty unusual rhythm section. As a result, I never got to do a lot of soloing live because when I stopped playing the bottom would pretty much fall out of the song.

When we were writing material for the *Muscle Of Love* album, we flew out to Los Angeles and stayed at the Malibu colony. It was here that we recorded some of the basic tracks with Bob Dolin and Mick Mashbir, who was a long time friend of Neal's from school. Sometimes Glen would come in and try to do some guitar parts. In the end, he didn't play on any of the basic tracks. To get around this, he was made to feel like a star, "Glen we'll put your tracks on separately". Bob worked with him a bit, some spoon things, some sound affects — "OK, Glen you're done". The main guitar tracks were done by Steve Hunter, Dick Wagner, Mick Mashbir, and myself.

The Malibu colony was really nice — a gated community with big boats and Cadillacs. It was there that we did the photo sessions with us wearing the sailor suits. We went out on this converted military vessel and took the photos of us peeling potatoes, etc. The academy of nude wrestling photos were taken at the building across the street from Sunset Sound on Sunset Boulevard.

Between some of the last shows we had a break and went up to Toronto for a couple of weeks. The attitude all along for *Muscle Of Love* had been, "fuck the stage show, let's do an album between shows — a non-concept album". Sort of like *Love It To Death* had been prior to the whole *Killer* concept taking over. The band just didn't want to do another full blown concept album. We had loosely worked up this idea based around sailors getting wild on shore leave — a vaguely sexual theme but that was about it. We thought that would be enough of a concept for the album and a short tour. Then we'd take a badly needed break. We were all pretty adamant about this, the band were putting their proverbial foot down. After all, we were big enough now, the *Billion Dollar Babies* album went to number 1, it felt like everyone in the world knew who the band was.

OK — first big snag — we get up to Toronto to Nimbus 9 studios and Bob wasn't in the studio. So we set up and started jamming on the riff to the song "Big Apple Dreaming". Well Bob had obviously been in the building somewhere — because he suddenly bursts out of the control room and says, "Wait, wait, that's not what you want to do — Neal you do this, and Michael you play this..." And everybody was looking at each other and thinking, "What the fuck? Can't he even take two seconds and say 'hello'? Can't we even discuss what we're playing?" Well instead he was barking out orders for a couple of hours and everybody was thinking "Fuck this". Finally Bob left. Supposedly he was having some sort of nervous breakdown and that's why he acted the way that he did and eventually couldn't produce the album. I think at the time he was going through a divorce. In the end Jack Richardson and Jack Douglas took over.

Muscle Of Love was the album I really held back on. I didn't really put a lot of effort into the writing. I remember Jack Richardson asking me, "What's going on with you Michael? Why aren't you writing any stuff? Come on quit being a slacker." He was like reprimanding me — trying to make me feel guilty. And I said, "Jack, I've just been holding back so the other guys could come up with some stuff", and he said, "Ah bullshit — you're a writer, so write".

Even though there was a definite intentional sexual theme that ran throughout the album, I think what was missing from *Muscle Of Love* was the thread that tied the whole thing together. This was partly due to the fact that we didn't have Bob Ezrin working with us. But I actually liked the *Muscle Of Love* record, even though we didn't have a lot of time to record it. I didn't think there was anything wrong with it. I wasn't crazy about all the production. It felt to me like we had really lost our hard edge — all those creamy slide solos by Mick Mashbir. They were great — don't get me wrong — but not like the old albums with Glen. Besides we always knew that *Billion Dollar Babies* was going to be a hard act to follow.

"Woman Machine" was another song like "Reflected". Back during The Spiders days we had a song called "Mister Machine"— we rewrote it and thought "Woman Machine" was kind of a comment on Helen Reddy's "I Am Woman", a song which was also out at the time. Also it's about an inflatable doll.

"Big Apple Dreaming (Hippo)" was kind of our disco song. It had a real dance feel to it. The Hippo was this big dance club in New York. The song was sort of a reflection on Alice hanging out at all the clubs in New York. Another show-orientated song.

"Never Been Sold Before" was written when Mick Mashbir came to the studio. Alice wrote the lyrics about some prostitute. They used this song during the opening credits to the ill-fated Alice Cooper movie *Good To See You Again, Alice Cooper.*

"Hard Hearted Alice" was a song I wrote after everyone had finally moved out of the Galecie Estate completely. Neal got a place in Westport, Connecticut. Dennis and Cindy got their own place. I also got my own place on Honeyridge Road with Bob Dolin and Mick Mashbir. That was kind of my first shot at stepping out from the band, the three of us used to jam a lot. Anyway "Hard Hearted Alice" was one of those songs where the music and words just flowed right out together. I think it was really about the band — I think my intuition was telling me that the band was breaking up. Alice also added some of the lyrics, classic "Coop" style.

"Crazy Little Child" was a song I had first written in high school. But of course, the final version turned out very different. For a start we didn't use Neal's original drum tracks. Initially he had played something with a very heavy feel to it, but later Jack Richardson had his band's drummer re-do the tracks. Jack had his own band that played big band and Dixieland jazz. So he really got into this track and challenged us to play it his way. A lot of the time we would record tracks and Jack would make a lot of changes in the studio. I don't think Neal felt particularly comfortable playing the song the way it turned out, let's face it this was a real step outside the normal Alice Cooper material.

"Working Up A Sweat" was another tune I had and it was basically a song about masturbation. Alice wrote some lyrics — I originally came up with the

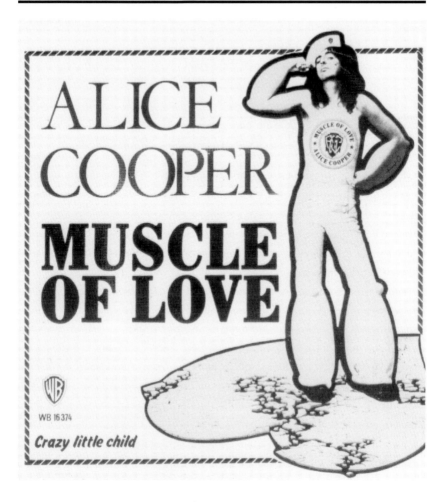

chorus first. I used to write choruses first and then the verses would come. It was a good song. No "Under My Wheels", but still good.

The title track "Muscle Of Love" was a real Alice Cooper song. I wrote all the music and Alice wrote some good lyrics to it. I think he came up with the title "Muscle Of Love".

I tend to think that "Teenage Lament" was the wrong song to release as the first single. It was a song that Neal wrote. It wasn't that it was a bad song, it was actually a very catchy tune, one of Neal's best. But again it was like "Hello Hooray" a big schmaltzy production deal with Liza Minnelli, the Pointer sisters, Patti Labelle and Ronnie Spector singing backing vocals. But did the kids really care about the fact that it was Liza Minnelli? I think it would have been good second single but "Muscle Of Love" should have been the first.

Incidentally, Alice had been introduced to Liza Minnelli by our set designer Joe Gannon. Joe had previously worked on lighting for Minnelli's show and he told us that she was apparently a fan of the group.

While in England we'd been approached by some people who asked us if we'd like a shot at writing the theme song to next Bond movie *The Man With The Golden Gun*. The whole band were big James Bond fanatics and jumped at the chance to do it. With our love of soundtracks and showbiz, I guess we were looking forward to hearing our song playing over the distinctive opening credits.

So we wrote this song specifically for the James Bond movie. Unfortunately it never made it into the film. They passed on our song and used Lulu's instead. I still think our song was fucking great.

Muscle of Love was released at the end of 1973 and I think the public was expecting another Alice Cooper band concept album. In retrospect what they got was really the sound of a band trying something different. Our mutation from dirty kick ass rock 'n' rollers to a slick showbiz band was now complete, but it was a transition that had left us in serious need of some time off. Our dilemma was neatly summed up by Lenny Kaye's review of the album which described: "Part of the problem is conceptual. *Muscle of Love* is the first album since Alice's early efforts that doesn't centre around a complete stage routine or vaguely fleshed-out fantasy. The Cooper experience as a whole has seldom been song-orientated, rather relying on its cumulative image impact. As a result *Muscle Of Love*, a collection of tracks, has a curiously hazy feel, in which various facets of the group's concerns are laid out then left for the listener to sort into place. The album's packaging mirrors this, a series of nice ideas that never seem to fully mesh."

In fact the sleeve was one of the things that really killed the *Muscle Of Love* album. That damn cardboard box for an album cover. The idea was supposed to be a bit like John and Yoko's *Two Virgins* album which had come with brown paper wrapped around the cover. Ours was a plain brown box with the words "enclosed — one muscle of love" printed on it. The idea was — what's inside here? It's a mystery. But what happened was the album wasn't well received by the distributors because there were only twelve records to each carton and it was difficult to fit into the album racks in the stores. In some countries like Brazil they got rid of the cardboard box altogether and turned the inside picture sleeve of the academy of nude wrestling into the cover of the record.

I guess Warner Bros were getting a bit concerned. Our two previous albums had shifted over a million copies in the first week. *Muscle Of Love* only sold about 800,000, so it fell a little bit short of their expectations, and to make matters worse, it wasn't followed up with a major worldwide stage show.

By the time we got to thinking about taking the *Muscle Of Love* songs out on tour, Glen was really sick and in a bad way. The rest of the band started having conversations about why Alice wasn't showing up for rehearsals. We realised that essentially Alice didn't want to turn up because he had to deal with Glen. It was obvious we were going to have to do something about it. I remember finally one day in a last ditch effort to save the band. Neal, Alice and I confronted Glen about his problems. Pretty much I did most of the talking. I said to Glen, "Look the band isn't happening. A lot of it has to do with your inability to deal with your problems. We're still going to pay you your twenty percent, but your guitar playing isn't cutting it. We want you to start taking guitar lessons". So, Glen took some guitar lessons — jazz guitar lessons — a lot of good that did! We also insisted that Glen did something about his drinking.

So, before we did the final tour we checked Glen into a rehab hospital back in Phoenix and got Mick Mashbir to come out from Arizona to play guitar. Mick had originally just come out to fill in for Glen during rehearsals. The idea was that when Glen came back he would replace Mick. With that in mind we gave Glen a tape of the new material to learn whilst he was in rehab. Occasionally, we would check in on him and ask, "Are you learning the new songs?" And he'd say "Oh, yeah man." So when he got out of the hospital we thought he had learned the new songs — well he hadn't learned any of them. It was apparent to everybody that he wasn't going to be able to pull his guitar parts off. So we kept Mick on for the tour. Mick already knew the material — we had no choice. I think Glen resented that, but it was his own fault.

Although I feel Glen really contributed to the demise of the group, we were never actually trying to get rid of him. We were always trying to keep the formula alive. But Glen was forever showing up drunk and disorderly. On those rare occasions Alice would be doing an interview with the band around, Glen would start talking shit. By the *Muscle Of Love* tour, Glen was on stage

Above: The cover from the "Only Women Bleed" sheet music. The photo featured the original band from 1971, and most copies had to be destroyed.

but most of the time he wasn't plugged into the house speakers. He could only be heard on "I'm Eighteen" and "School's Out", after all they were his riffs. The rest of the time all the audience could hear was Mick Mashbir on lead guitar — you could only hear Glen in our stage monitors. As a result we tried to keep Glen away from hearing any mixes of the shows. It was really a sad state of affairs. Glen would start and stop wrong, be out of tune, you name it. He really started to deteriorate.

Then, one day towards the end of the final tour, we were all in the limo waiting to go. Glen was up in the hotel room and wouldn't come out. We all pounded on the door and tried to get him to come out. Finally Dave Leibert, our road manager, tried to kick the door down. Well, Glen finally opened it and pulled a knife on Dave, so we all got back in the limo and went to the airport without Glen. He caught a later flight, but from that point on Glen didn't travel with the band.

For the *Muscle Of Love* shows, Shep said, "We have got to have some gimmick for the new show". And we were going, "Why?" My opinion was that I didn't think anyone would have been that disappointed if there weren't a lot of theatrics for the tour — I could have been wrong. In the end we carried on with the *Billion Dollar Babies* stage. In effect this short tour wasn't really a *Muscle of Love* tour, but an extension of the previous one, we just added some of the new songs into the show.

The cannon idea was a last minute desperate attempt to introduce a new element of theatricality to the show. It was another Amazing Randi stunt from vaudeville. The general idea was that Alice would get inside this large cannon by climbing down inside the barrel. Then he would escape through a trap door at the bottom and get out of the cannon. A dummy would then be placed inside the barrel. Gunpowder and flash chargers would ignite causing a spring to shoot the dummy out of the cannon over the audience. And then Alice would reappear somewhere — but it never worked properly. We were trying to figure out something else that might work — I thought one idea would be for Alice to get on top of the cannon and stroke it. Then the cannon would shoot a foamy wad out over the audience, but unfortunately that didn't work either, it just dripped out the end of the barrel.

So now we were becoming overladen with problems. We were promoting an LP which wasn't selling like it should, we had a guitarist that wasn't travelling with the band or plugged in at concerts, and we had a distinct lack of any gimmick to sell the show. All this was compounded by the problems we were already having on the tour due to the winter fuel embargo and truck strike. The trucker's strike came about because of the fuel rationing which was introduced when the United States were getting pressed by the Middle East. The truckers were allocated a set amount of gasoline and there were long lines in Los Angeles and all over the country.

For some of the shows we would get to the arena and the stage never turned up at all. We managed to rent some gear, but after the first few times that happened it was really frustrating. So, not only were there no theatrics, but we would have to play on a completely flat stage. Neal wouldn't even have a drum riser to play on. But in a way it was like getting back to basics, and I kind of liked playing like that. I remember we did this show with Flo & Eddie in Maine. It was the last gig before we went to Brazil and we even performed "A Hard Days Night" for our encore. Flo & Eddie came out on stage and sang it with us. Despite all the problems, we still sold out most of the shows on the final tour.

I think there were signs that our reputation for confrontation was beginning to backfire on us. Things came to a head at the Toledo Sports Arena where we were billed to play to a sell out crowd of 8,000 fans. During ZZ Top's support set, the crowd started to chuck fireworks about. The general pushing and shoving in the front rows meant that by the time we hit the stage, missiles were being thrown everywhere. Our PR manager was quoted as saying that the crowd seemed to be "more bewildered than angry at anything". The story then given to the press was that a firework had hit one of the overhead lights which shattered and I was hit in the face by flying glass. The show was then cancelled. They even said that later that night in hospital a particle of metal had to be removed from my eye.

What really happened was that somebody threw an M80 and it blew up and they took us off stage. The security was so bad that Shep didn't want the gig to go ahead, so we got out of it by saying that I was hurt. I was banished to my hotel room and in the paper the next day it said "Cooper guitarist injured by blast", but that never really happened.

But increasingly bizarre incidents were beginning to haunt the band. We had caused some controversy in Calgary where it was reported that a 13 year old boy had hung himself in his bedroom in what was described as a rash of "Cooper-inspired hanging parties". Apparently after the airing of an *In Concert* programme, the boy had boasted that Alice's act was an illusion which he could duplicate. This led to a game of dares where the boy strung himself from the ceiling and jumped off a chair. Apparently he had done it before with no problem. This time his game had obviously gone seriously wrong. The result was that the local Coroner's report called for a ban on TV programmes where mock violent acts like hanging were shown in graphic detail.

Playing in Brazil also had its hairy moments, but was a particularly memorable experience. We arrived at the airport and the promoter picked us up in a Lear jet. We flew to the hotel and it was like The Beatles arriving. They took us to the show in jeeps with machine guns on them. They drove us down the wrong side of the freeway to get us there, all the other vehicles had to pull over to the side of the road. When we got to the show there were 125,000 people indoors, a record attendance which got us into the Guinness Book of Records. As they hadn't had too many concerts down there, the security wasn't all it could've been and people started pushing more and more towards the stage. By about the third number the people were trying to clamour up onto the front of the stage, just piling on top of one another until they were almost up to the top of this ten foot stage. Finally the police got up there with machine guns and stopped the show by firing their guns into the air. Everything stopped for fifteen or twenty minutes while they tried to regain order by getting everyone to sit down again. We started again about half an hour later.

That night we went to this club about three o'clock in the morning, and one of the roadies spots this big beautiful black chick. So he's all hot for her on the dance floor, dancing with this chick. He wanted to take her back to the hotel, even though everyone warned him not to mess with her. The night wears on and we get this big booth in the corner and everyone is shit-faced drunk, and this guy is all over this chick. So he sticks his hand under her dress and there's a dick there. Well all of a sudden the guy's face turns two shades pale and he looks real uncomfortable. He freaked. But I must admit this guy/chick was beautiful, it was an easy mistake to make.

Alice Cooper, solo star, was really born around the time of *Muscle Of Love*. Little by little he started spending less time with the band. I got the distinct impression that Alice thought the band was becoming an embarrassment to him and we were cramping his style. He was in a different league now. Sometimes it wasn't so bad, but other times it felt awkward being around him. There were times when the band would make an appearance and everyone would ignore us. They just wanted to take pictures and talk with Alice. We felt like we might as well have been wallpaper. Alice was increasingly hanging out with a new set of friends whose opinion seemed to be, "Hey Alice, you're the star — you don't need those other guys". Neal also got an apartment in New York and hung out with Alice a bit. But even Neal wasn't part of Alice's new clique.

By this time, because we were all earning good money, we were becoming much more independent of each other anyway. There wasn't the same communal feeling there had been in the early days. After the *Muscle Of Love* tour, I took off and went to the islands. Then I went out to Arizona and invested in property. We were all starting to do our own thing. Alice and Shep were certainly doing their thing, pumping the press and media — "Alice did this, and Alice did that". Again they weren't discussing any of it with the band and all the decisions were being made by them. We felt that our dissatisfaction was understandable.

By now Glen was not only drinking really heavily but also getting into heavy drugs — something which I didn't even know at the time. That's when the whole thing really started to fall apart. It got to the situation where quite often we would be rehearsing without Alice, but he was still off doing all the interviews and stuff. *Rolling Stone* would come out with his picture on it, or in *Creem* magazine the article would just be about him; no mention of the band. We would question Shep about this and he would say, "Everything's OK".

Alice was correct in that *Rolling Stone* interview — yes, the band wanted to try something different — mainly it was me and Neal wanting to do solo LPs. We had already agreed that after *Muscle Of Love* we would take some time off. Everybody was tired — things were not going well. We all needed some time to ourselves. We had been recording and touring virtually non-stop for four years. But when I originally presented the solo LP idea to Shep, I didn't want to stop the band, I simply said, "Look if we're going to take some time off, I'd like to do a record of my own". I suppose if I had gotten a big smash hit with my solo record I might have done what Alice did — I don't know. But I like to think I would have still carried on with the band.

Occasionally they would throw us a bone. For instance I had been approached by Gibson and made a deal with them to manufacture the Michael Bruce anniversary guitar — based on the white SG I used to play then. Well Joe and Shep go, "Well, what about strings and accessories? Let's get everything we can from them". So Gibson got irritated with this and said, "Fuck it". I lost the deal — believe me I was pissed off.

This was par for the course for the way management ran things. Later, when Alice quit, Shep goes, "I can't bring Alice back because you don't have an employment contract with him." So I said, "Well, gee Shep, that was your job". I'm sure he has a contract with everything he does now. When the band hit a sour note with *Muscle Of Love* I think Shep saw the writing on the wall. He took the attitude, "the band wants to do solo things — I'll take Alice and run...."

For their part, Glen and Dennis didn't want the band to do solo material — I think they sensed that if the band went down that road we would never get back together again. They were right of course, but at first we all fully intended to do a new album and tour. But underneath it all I think Alice had other plans. Shep warned us that after *Muscle Of Love*, "You guys better not take too much time off — the public forgets".

And I'd say, "I know, I just want to try and record some different things".

Shep was persistent, "I wouldn't advise you doing that Michael because once you open the door for Alice to do a solo thing he might not come back". How right he was.

I kept emphasizing, "Look I'm not looking to break-up the group, I just need the chance to do something on my own to clear my head."

Yet the thought from the management was still, "That's not a good idea". My response was that every fucking other band did it from Yes to the Grateful Dead, so why couldn't we? Dennis's philosophy for the group was that everybody should do their own thing within the format of Alice Cooper. Well, ideologically that was fine. But what was Alice Cooper? After a while everyone had their own idea of what Alice Cooper was. The main trouble was that it wasn't what the band wanted, or believed it to be. It was something management wanted it to be, or what Bob Ezrin's concept of the band was. The real payback was that by me and Neal doing solo projects Alice was able to say, "Well, they did it first. It was their idea, so now I can do it."

For a while the film *Good To See You Again Alice Cooper* was supposed to help keep the band alive. I felt the beginning of the movie was kind of cool — the Hollywood producers trying to make us into something we weren't. At the end of the song "Lady Is A Tramp" we revolt and trash the stage. It was a kind of a parody of what was really happening to the band at the time. Shep pretty much came up with the idea for the movie. None of us knew that all those old Hollywood film clips were going to be inter-spliced with the concert footage. I felt the live footage wasn't that good — for the most part it was very difficult to see the band because of the poor lighting. If I remember rightly the whole project was paid for by Bob Guccione of *Penthouse* magazine. Unfortunately the movie only opened in Greenwich, Connecticut for a couple of nights and then closed. We also did a video for "Muscle Of Love" which never came out featuring us in prison outfits — it was like the Alice Cooper group stage a jailbreak.

Then the *Greatest Hits* album came out. By now I was living in Lake Tahoe recording solo material. Alice was living in Los Angeles. Shep wound up getting me a deal with Polydor Germany for my solo album which was entitled *In My Own Way.*

Glen, Neal, and Dennis were still in Connecticut. Neal and Dennis were working on Neal's solo album *Platinum God* which never got released in the end. It was a concept Neal had been working on, Dennis played all the bass, and Neal wrote and sang all the songs. He even got the New York Philharmonic to do some orchestration. He took it around a lot of record companies, but coming from a band that played shock rock, it was far from what they were expecting. The title track, for instance, was an interesting mixture of modern and primitive drumming. Who knows, maybe some day it will be released.

Then Dennis and Neal did a project with Mike Marconi called The Flying Tigers. They eventually signed a deal with CBS records but that album also got shelved.

Looking back on it, the last nail in the Alice Cooper group coffin, was when Shep lost the lawsuit over the group's publishing. The whole problem had started way back when Herb Cohen sold us to Warners, right after the *Easy Action* record. Then the band immediately records our third album *Love It To Death* and boom we get a hit with "I'm Eighteen". Then Herbie goes, "Wait a minute, I just sold the band — I didn't sell the publishing". So Shep's furious and now starts the five year lawsuit. Warner Bros fronted us our royalty money as if there hadn't been a problem, so the band could continue on its merry way. In the meantime there wasn't much in the way of sheet music or songbooks around because the publishing was being fought over between Herb and Shep. So finally around the time of *Muscle Of Love*, the lawsuit comes to trial out

Above: "It's behind you!" For the Welcome To My Nightmare tour Alice took rock n' roll theatre to its extreme. *Photo: Phillip Hendrix.*

in LA. I think Dennis and Alice were called down to testify. Well, Shep was infuriated because he found out that the attorneys he had hired, who were on retainers all those years, hadn't done shit for the case. Shep looked at the file and there was hardly anything there. So he fired them.

The outcome was that Shep lost the lawsuit. Herbie got the publishing for *Pretties For You, Easy Action, Love It To Death, Killer, School's Out* and *Billion Dollar Babies*, and Shep got *Muscle Of Love* and the *Greatest Hits* — that's all he got after all those years of work. Shep was saying, "What the fuck do I have now? I've got to start all over again with these guys — and the band's flaking out". *Muscle Of Love* wasn't selling like the previous records and then there were the problems with Glen, and the tour not going so well. So then... ahhhh, all of sudden the solo idea. Shep starts saying things along the lines of, "If you do this Michael, I can't be responsible for Alice". All of a sudden the doors are open and Shep walks right through — takes Bob Ezrin with him and on down the road with Alice they go. So after the *Nightmare* LP and tour was a success, Shep starts signing up publishing deals with Blondie, Pure Prairie League, New Riders of The Purple Sage — even Racquel Welsh. Just recently he sold his publishing to Sony.

I remember reading an interview with Shep and the question was, "What was your biggest disappointment?" And Shep goes "that the *Muscle Of Love* album wasn't a hit". But to me the whole thing looked a bit neat. It was all rather convenient to let this album take the fall and then put a bad rap on the group. I sometimes wonder if Bob really had a nervous breakdown or not, maybe he just didn't want to do the album. Or, maybe they just thought that they'd take Alice and run. I don't know if they were that scheming or not, or it just worked out that way.

In any event, after the band did their solo LPs in 1974, Shep said he wouldn't come back to the band. I always thought he should have taken a stronger stance for the group as a whole and not just let things go like that. When Shep told me, "Alice doesn't want to come back to the group" I think Shep should have said, "You guys don't have an employment agreement — you better get one if you ever hope to have Alice back because that's the only thing that's going to stop him." Yet Shep jumped right on Alice's bandwagon and made it all possible for Alice to go solo. Basically, if Shep hadn't helped Alice, we probably would have gotten back together.

I think that the material for *In My Own Way*, my solo record, was good. (Recently re-issued on CD on One Way in the US). Looking back on it, a lot of that music was written out of frustration. I was so disenchanted after *Muscle Of Love* I would have tried anything. I just wanted to do it on my own and it didn't matter what it was. Anyway, I had my four demos done for my solo project with Jack Richardson — "King Of America", "Oh My Love" "Rock Rolls On" and "Nothing On Earth". They were done with Bob Dolin and Mick Mashbir. That's what I had submitted to Warner Bros to try and get a solo deal — well they passed on my stuff, Neal's stuff and even Alice's early demos. They wanted the Alice Cooper group, not solo stuff. Warner Bros had been in the business a long time and had probably seen this before. No doubt, they were thinking, "We'll have to promote these guys all over again, or can Alice do it on his own?"

Keith Moon came down to the Record Plant in 1974 when I was recording my solo record. Dino Dinelli (from The Rascals) invited him down to play on the album. So Keith Moon came down and got shit-faced drunk — he had drunk two bottles of Napoleon brandy before he even played. I was in the control booth listening to him play the song. Although he played the drums great, he was completely out of synch with the music. At first I asked the engineers, "What kind of delay do you have on the drums?", because it sounded like he was playing the song perfect but a note or two behind the beat. And the engineers said, "there's no delay, that's how he's playing it." Moon was so drunk he heard the music in a different tempo. But I did use some of his tracks on the "Rock Rolls On" cut. He reminded me of a kid with a lot of sugar in his system.

Also, while I was at the Record Plant, who staggers in but old Harry Nilsson again. Nilsson was then one of a select bunch of drinkers called the Hollywood Vampires that included John Lennon, Keith Moon and Alice that would hang around Hollywood and generally go on drinking binges in the top loft room of the Rainbow Club. Anyway, it was like Nilsson picked up where he last left off, running his mouth off. Again I don't know why. I was ready to deck him then also.

Alice even came down and sang on my solo record, but he was keeping his own solo album very secret. I remember vaguely discussing his solo project with him at that time. Then a few months later he invites me down to the soundstage at Warner Bros — I saw the whole trip — the dancers and costumes, the whole *Welcome To My Nightmare* show. It was then that I knew it was over because he was doing the whole Alice Cooper show without the band. Then Atlantic signed Alice for the *Welcome To My Nightmare* album. Shep told me that to get the deal Bob Ezrin went into Warner Bros and played songs from every album from *Love It To Death* through to *Billion Dollar Babies*. He even played them some of the stuff off *Muscle Of Love* which he didn't produce. Then boom — he got the deal for Alice because he showed them what he could do. To me, it all seemed a mighty quick recovery from that nervous breakdown!

I attribute much of the break-up purely to the fact that everything was being handled badly. The band wasn't able to seek its own course anymore — other people started making all the decisions. "We know what's right for the band" they'd say and it all fell apart. And the world wasn't holding its breath for us to get it together, so guess what — here comes this group Kiss. They know what they're doing and how to do it. They don't need one guy with make-up — they got four guys with make-up — four Alice's. We couldn't even control the one Alice we had! I can remember as far back as late 1971 the guys in Kiss were early fans of the group and originally did an Alice Cooper tribute show. Shep had to tell them to quit or he would sue them. They just took the whole thing a step further — along with the merchandising. But I think we were more original with our stage show and songwriting.

I did see the *Nightmare* show which I thought was good except for the band being behind the screen. I don't think the band themselves thought it was too hot, but I think Alice didn't want anyone to know who was in the band — who knows? Funny that the original sheet music for the single "Only Women Bleed" featured a picture of the old group and subsequently had to be destroyed. Anyway, I remember going backstage and looking at all those female dancers that Alice had hired. All I could think was that I would rather be dating them than doing a gig with them. And then of course there were all the golf clubs hanging around. Golf was becoming a major love of Alice's.

Even after the *Nightmare* LP, Alice never really said it was over until finally we had our lawyers meet and talk when he played in Michigan at Cobo Hall. So we got together and settled up for the name, were supposed to get 3% of everything he did with the name after *Nightmare*. Shep said we didn't have an employment contract so we couldn't force Alice to come back into the group so that was it, the band had disbanded because we had no Alice. So we lost our contract with Warner Bros. And the rest of us were out of a record deal and a lot of money too. It was well and truly over. I think that Alice had decided to move on. We had to be philosophical about it. Bands have always broken up — just look at The Beatles.

Battle Axe and Beyond

In the end I couldn't get a solo deal in America even though I had sold my *In My Own Way* album to Polygram Germany for $30,000. But they weren't going to release it until I got a Stateside deal which never happened. I should have released it myself but at that time I was very confused. By recording a solo album I had got a lot of things out of my system and it was only then that I saw the writing on the wall. OK, so maybe I had never really received the recognition I thought I deserved, but who was I without the band?

After a year or so drifting around trying to launch solo careers, Dennis, Neal and myself decided to get back together and form a band. I think we had all grown up a bit. Neal and Dennis wanted to get something going. And so we formed the Billion Dollar Babies. Nobody seemed to mind us using the name. We were joined by keyboard player Bob Dolin and guitarist Mike Marconi. I had heard Mike Marconi play and the energy excited me.

I remember going into New York on the train and we were talking about a good, tough, ballsy rock 'n' roll title for the album and we hit upon *Battle Axe*. *Rollerball* was the big movie out at the time we thought let's make it a sport. We went through the whole evolutionary thing of developing a concept, like the old days except this time without Alice and Glen. Neal, Dennis and I just brainstormed the hell out of it and came up with a great idea. *Battle Axe* was this futuristic time in society when the ultimate spectacle was a rock 'n' roll sports event — sort of jock rock. Countries would be represented by rock 'n' roll groups that would fight to the death for money and power. It was a sort of rock 'n' roll version of *Gladiators*. A big scoreboard in the back would flash the scores. Before the band would come on stage a backing tape of NFL music would play. Real ancient Roman coliseum-type music.

Then, during the song "Ego Mania", Marconi and I would joust and fight, trading guitar leads back and forth. We would be wearing these helmets, shoulder pads, and breast plates — sort of like futuristic American football players. I would knock Mike Marconi down twice and then we would be in "sudden death". While Marconi was down I would turn to the audience and hold my thumb up and then down and they would cheer. Then I would go pick up "the battle axe" — it was a like a plexi-glass clear guitar with a chrome bayonet. Smoke would rise above the stage. We bought fifty cheap Japanese guitars and cut them with a saw so when you whacked one against something it would shatter into pieces. (The same idea was later used by Black Oak Arkansas who featured a section in their show where the two guitarists would battle it out with cheap Japanese guitars).

Of course the plan was that we would also do some of the Alice Cooper songs during the *Battle Axe* show. We started with "Hello Hooray" and then into "Billion Dollar Babies", then "Under My Wheels", "18" "Elected", we also encored with "Schools Out". Each one of us took a personal loan of $30,000 out of our bank accounts to get the show on the road so to speak. In the end we only did four shows, Flint (Michigan), where we tried it out. Muskeegan (Illinois), Pontiac (MI), and the last show we headlined with Michael Schenker and UFO. Supposedly once the record was released we were going to do these 5,000 seater shows promoted by Concerts West (who promoted the Rolling Stones and The Who) but this never happened.

One of the problems was the record itself. When Lee Decarlo mixed it, he was under a lot of strain and pressure and also we were over budget. During mix-down he really cranked the high end so that on the finished record the needle literally leaped right out of the grooves. As a result albums were getting returned. It was clear we had an emergency on our hands and we ended up spending a further $12,000 of our own money to go back into the studio to remix the album with Jack Richardson. The record was then released again — but it was pretty much too late — the damage was done. Not surprisingly the *Battle Axe* album didn't chart like it should have done — it never recovered even though they shipped 60,000 records. So the booking agents weren't interested even though we did get on TV and were featured in some pretty big magazines, but that wasn't enough. The promotional side of things wasn't properly taken care of either. I think Leo Fenn was trying to prove that he was instrumental in breaking the band, and in a way, he was. But unfortunately he didn't have Shep's charisma.

In the end Polydor records were saying, "We've just spent $100,000 and we've got nothing to show for it. We're not going to spend anymore money". We had this huge stage we couldn't afford to haul around. With the tour collapsing we couldn't afford to put the show on. The stage sat in a warehouse and finally we had to let it go. Dennis in particular was disappointed in the way the Billion Dollar Babies band fell apart, especially as he was the one who'd said we should have gone for a less ambitious, more practical stage show — and he was right because it turned around and bit us on the ass.

I guess maybe the whole idea of overblown rock theatre was becoming outdated. In England punk had created a shock wave. Even though some of the punk bands were supposedly influenced by the original Alice Cooper group, I never cared too much for it. I thought it was too disorganised, disorderly and destructive. The stuff that we did had a kind of message to it. I don't know whether it was as clear to the people who watched it. But we'd have the different parts of the show, it definitely wasn't all dark or negative, there was a light and very positive side. A lot of the punk bands would just come on and play as loud as they could and yell "motherfucker" for an hour and a half. That sort of thing gets tired and boring really quickly and I don't think anyone in the band cared for that.

While things had been going right for the band it just seemed to make such perfect sense. For a while it all seemed so clear. Then when it all started coming apart, disco and punk started happening, the few gigs that we tried to do, nobody was interested, it was like all of a sudden, you were there, and then you're passed by. America's real famous for trends. People see a way to make money by promoting something. The big record companies went cold on the glam bands — onto the next big thing they could make money from I guess. But our time had come and gone.

So Neal, Dennis and I disbanded the Billion Dollar Babies. At the time I was engaged to this girl in New Jersey, I was low on money and had to sell my house in Lake Tahoe. In the end it didn't work out and I moved back to Arizona, while Neal and Dennis stayed in Connecticut. Back in Arizona I set-

Above: Poster for the new Billion Dollar Babies.
Opposite top: The Josiah Bruce Band
Opposite bottom: The new Billion Dollar Babies - Lan Nichols, myself, my brother Paul Bruce and Ant-Bee. *Photo: Charlotte James*

tled down and married my first wife Kelly and we raised three kids.

As regards relations with Alice himself, after the whole *Nightmare* scene, Alice's mom called me up and said, "Alice would like to work with you again", so I called him up and somehow I missed him and he never got back in touch. I don't know what happened. I did go backstage to one of his shows in 1978 during his greatest hits tour based around *Lace & Whiskey*. I was told he wanted to see me. So we went up to his dressing room and waited. Then his parents came in. My first wife and I were shuffled to another room. So we were waiting in there all by ourselves. Finally we left without me ever getting a chance to talk to him.

I remember a couple of years after that Kelly and I took Alice's wife Sherryl to dinner. We took her to the Camelback restaurant in Phoenix. She was driving their old Rolls Royce — it was the same car he finally sold at the Barrett car auction out in LA. Anyway she told us that she had left Alice until he cleaned up his act. I guess this was when he was going through a really dark phase and drinking really heavily — even his dad thought Alice was going to die. In a way, we all paid a heavy price for fame. I think everybody in the band became a victim of their own vices. I know I later became a victim of mine. I got into some things I shouldn't have and it really screwed me up too. In the end Alice checked into the Betty Ford Clinic and gave up drinking. Sherryl and him have been together ever since and have three kids.

Sadly, things went from bad to worse for Glen. By this time he had eventually worked his way back to Arizona. I heard sometime later that he had tried to kill himself. What is certain is that he lost his house to the IRS. He then married and moved to Iowa.

Later on I remember Kelly seeing Alice in 1981 in Scottsdale, Arizona. Alice had set his parents up with this store where they sold fake Indian stuff which was eventually fire bombed destroying $200,000 of stock and some of Alice's gold records. His parents told her that Alice wanted to talk to me so I gave him a call and he said to me jokingly, "So do the rest of the guys still want to beat me up", we both laughed. So we talked about doing something together — the spark was still there. Then he went and saw Dennis and Neal. So it looked like a reunion might follow. Then Alice went to Toronto to talk with Bob Ezrin and he refused to work with any of us — as I understand it, he thought we weren't good enough musicians. Can you believe that?

Then around 1982, I sent Alice some songs to consider recording. One was "Hostage Of Your Love" the other was "Gina" which wound up on my second solo LP, *Rock Rolls On*. I didn't really care much about the lyrics — we could have changed them — but the music was real strong. In the end *Rock Rolls On* was released on an independent label called Eurotech. It featured versions of songs from the *In My Own Way* album. There were also some new songs like "Do You Wanna Know" which I co-wrote with Neal who was featured along with Dennis and Bob Dolin. Unfortunately this mini-album had very limited distribution and promotion, so it went nowhere.

Then in the early 1990s I met this black dude, Josiah — that kind of rekindled the spark — we formed the Josiah/Bruce band. He sang sort of like Alice. Then, in 1994 I began working and recording with Ant-Bee (Billy James) who helped me put this book together. We worked on a song called "Return of the Titanic Overture" (recorded at Cape Fear Studios, NC) which featured on the Ant-Bee CD *Lunar Muzik* (Divine Records, UK). I wrote the music and Billy wrote some lyrics. I played the keyboards, bass, and guitars and Billy produced it, sang all the vocals, played drums and tape manipulations. It's a sort of tribute to the original Alice Cooper group and the "Titanic Overture" theme from *Pretties For You* resurfaces. Also, there are excerpts reworked by Billy of Neal's "Platinum God" song. Neal, Glen, Dennis and myself are featured on several other tracks and it was the first time the Alice Cooper group without Alice had been recorded together in twenty years.

I'm also featured quite extensively on some other Ant-Bee material like the CD single "Child Of The Moon" (Divine, UK). On it there is a demo of a song I wrote back during the *Pretties For You* days called "Come With Us Now". The original Alice Cooper group performed this live at the Whiskey back in 1969 but never recorded it. I sang and played the keyboards and slide guitar. Billy sang background vocals and played percussion. It was recorded at Flux Audio Video, Wilmington, North Carolina, and engineered by Pat Ogelvie. In May 1995 we played a benefit concert in Wilmington and recorded a live version of "I'm Eighteen" which is featured on the CD single as well. Also, we recorded a new version of "Living" (from *Pretties For You*) which is featured on Ant-Bee's album *Electronic Church Muzik*. There is a cover version of "Sick Things" by the group Antiseen, led by Jeff Clayton, on which I played a guitar solo. It appeared on their album *Here To Ruin Your Groove* (SPV/Rebel Records, Germany — Baloney Shrapnel Records, USA).

Above: Michael Bruce and Ant-Bee onstage with the new Billion Dollar Babies in Charlotte, NC, November 1995.

Opposite top: After the break-up of the Alice Cooper Group, Neal Smith started a successful real estate company.

Opposite bottom: Michael Bruce meets Tesla backstage

Specializing in Westport, Weston & Wilton

When you decide to buy or sell your home in Westport, Weston or Wilton, you want a real estate agent who really knows all three communities. And few realtors can match the combination of professional expertise and personal experience that Neal offers.

As a member of both the Westport/Weston and Wilton Boards of Realtors, Neal specializes in listing and selling properties in all three towns. In fact, he's been selling and investing in local property — professionally and personally — since 1975. And, as a current resident of Wilton, and former resident of Westport and Weston, he personally knows just about everything there is to know about each of these lovely communities.

Add to that Neal's experience with national relocation — plus his affiliation with an international real estate agency — and you've got an unbeatable combination for unbeatable results!

Then I formed a new Billion Dollar Babies band and gigged up and down the East coast. It was just basic rock 'n' roll without the snakes. The new group consisted of me on guitars and vocals, Ant-Bee on drums, Lan Nichols on bass and Paul Bruce (my brother) on keyboards, and sometimes Ronnie Newman on bass and Rob N' Pillage on guitar. Also Rod Martin as our sound guy and Wayne Langston as roadie. We did an assortment of new material and the old Cooper classics.

I also continued writing and recording material with the hope of getting a possible new album out. One of my recent songs "Man Without A Heart" has to do with the feeling about going through a broken marriage. It also dealt with some of the situations in my then marriage where I felt torn between wanting to get back into music in a big way and wanting to have a domestic life. I guess it's the classic struggle between the artist and the home body. It's a song about feeling kind of lost. I was going to send it to Alice to see if he would be interested in doing it on his next record.

At that time, I guess I still held some resentment toward Alice because he was the star and we weren't. But the whole band helped to create the aura that will always surround the name Alice Cooper. Of course this doesn't mean he wasn't talented — he wrote some great songs — but he was more of a lyricist. We used to sit down and I would play him stuff and then he'd get ideas for lyrics or I'd give him lyrics and he'd work with them. We worked well together, but many of those original Alice Cooper tracks were my songs. I think most people still think "Is It My Body" or "Be My Lover" is Alice writing about himself — but those are songs about me — not Alice. They just happened to fit in with the image of him that the band projected. But in reality I'd like to think that we were all the stars. Many people think the music we wrote together with the group was the best. Undoubtedly, Alice has made a living out of his solo career and done well. For a long time he wasn't interested in any sort of idea of reforming the band.

Rock Rolls On

In March 1996 after touring and working with Ant-Bee on various projects, I decided to return to Phoenix, Arizona, a move which coincided with splitting up with my second wife Amy.

After the first edition of this book was published, there were mixed feelings in the Alice camp. I know Alice himself wasn't happy with the book. I didn't really expect him to be in total agreement. I remember reading that Alice had said that he had read a couple of pages, and his comment was that he didn't know which category to file the book under — fact or fiction. I was wondering how he could make that kind of summation if he'd only read three or four pages. I assume he was referring to the fact that I speculated about the motivations surrounding the group's break-up. Because Alice and Shep hadn't really communicated with us a lot, sometimes we had to fill in the blanks ourselves. I'm sure Alice doesn't worry about everything he says in an interview — or check with all the other band members to see if it's all correct for that matter. I remember Neal read it and he said he thought it was about 90% correct.

There was a great reaction from fans — a lot of people liked the book, although I do remember people saying that Glen was a little upset by it. But in typical Glen Buxton style he got over it and said, "Yeh, that's true — that's how I was then." He hated to admit it, but he knew he was that way.

As for Dennis, I never really heard a reaction from him about the book, even though I went out of my way to give him the credit and recognition I think he

Top and middle left: Myself and Glen at Billy's Blues Club Houston, 10th October 1997.

Bottom left: The full Billy's Blues line-up, Neal Smith, myself, Richie Scarlet and Glen Buxton.

Above top: Neal cracks a joke. *Photo Laurie Jatras*

Above and right: Two shots from the infamous "Bikes & Babes" photo session.

All other photos: Dave Lovelace, courtesy of Torn Ticket Productions

deserved but never really received. However, Dennis is a quiet, private person so that's not that unusual.

The *In My Own Way* album was finally issued on CD by One-Way Records, USA, featuring one extra song from the original sessions called "Morning Song" which had never previously been available. I wish it had done better back when I recorded it, because I think it would probably have helped me out more now — as I really didn't have anything besides what the Cooper band did. A lot of people wondered why I hadn't done more of the Cooper style thing. But that was the whole point of doing it. At the time I was trying to get away from the Cooper stuff because we'd been doing that night and day for so long. The idea wasn't that this was to be my solo album and the end of the Cooper career — it was supposed to be in addition to it.

When it came to pressing the CD, I wasn't really happy with the safety masters (the master tapes were long since lost). I was disappointed to notice that when I played it against several other CDs, it wasn't as bright or clear and was kind of dull in comparison. Also, the overall level was low. But I think the music still stands up, I think it sounds very good.

In the summer/fall of 1996, I worked on new material in Phoenix. In February 1997, I got a call from Scott Rowe about a guy who lived in Houston and was a big fan of the Cooper group — his name was Jeff Jatras. He was willing to pay my way to Houston to play a gig with Scott Rowe's group. So I said, "sure". What transpired was Jeff eventually became my manager. So I flew to Houston and practised with Scott Rowe's Alice Cooper tribute group and did two shows. Jeff and I struck up a friendship and he wanted to meet the other guys in the Cooper group. So we eventually linked up with Neal, Dennis and even Glen. I also did a book signing at Borders bookstore in Houston at that time which went over very well! As a matter of fact, Kip Winger did one as well and I actually sold and signed more copies then even he did! Which is pretty good for an unknown old guy like myself.

In March 1997, Jeff and I went to Connecticut and recorded two songs called "Left For Dead Meat" and "You Rock My World" featuring Richie Scarlet on bass. I'd met Richie one night when I went to see an old friend of mine, Ace Freehley from Kiss, play at a club in 1995. I heard that someone (Richie) in the band very much wanted to meet me. So I waited after the show at my hotel to meet up with the group, but they never showed. Later on I found out that they had decided to change hotels, so that's why we never linked up.

Someone told me that Richie was getting married so I sent him and Joanna a picture I had signed. Then later on, after my stint with Ant-Bee in March '96, I went to see Ace's group perform at a club in Raleigh. NC. I finally got to meet Richie and I even got up on stage and jammed with Ace, Richie and Peter Criss. After this, Richie and I remained good friends and have worked together on various projects.

The two tracks I recorded with Richie ended up being problematic. It had been really cold in Connecticut and I picked up a really bad cold — my head was all stuffed and I couldn't hear very well. So when I got back to Houston I listened to the tracks and there were a lot of things about it I just couldn't live with, so I tried to transfer it from 24-track reel to digital and there were some problems with that. Then the more I listened to the tracks the more I realised there was just a lot of stuff I wasn't going to be able to fix. So I decided to scrap them. I'm planning on re-cutting those tracks because they are good songs.

In March 1997, Jeff formed Torn Ticket Productions (his management company). I then worked up an acoustic set of the classic Cooper tunes and some new material, and did several gigs in the Houston area, as well as appearing on the local Houston radio show, *Stevens and Prewett*. I also did an acoustic show with Al Stewart. He was really nice, and very friendly. He liked the material and the Cooper group — we had a great time. I played acoustic versions of "Desperado", "Caught In A Dream", "Hard Hearted Alice", "No More Mr. Nice Guy", and "Schools Out".

In August '97, I tried to link up with Alice at a gig in Houston, but it never happened. Just before I got there someone had evidently shown Alice an e-mail of an interview I had done 6 months to a year previously. I guess Alice was mad at me and didn't want to see me. It might have been about the book as well — I'm not really sure. It's hard getting information second hand as I never got to speak to anyone directly. So I said, "fine" and left. Since then Alice and I are on much better working terms — maybe it was just getting it all aired out. We have "buried the hatchet", so to speak, and who knows maybe one day we'll write together again.

In September 1997 I played Piney Woodstock with Rick Derringer. Rick and I had a good time — we hadn't seen each other for years. We did several shows together in the early days, and of course he played on "Under My Wheels" and "Yeah, Yeah, Yeah" on the *Killer* album. He was the first outside

Above and below: Myself, Rockin' Reggie, Neal Smith, Dennis Dunaway at Glen Buxton's funeral. *Photos: Jeff Jatras/Torn Ticket Productions*

GLEN E. BUXTON

November 10, 1947   October 19, 1997
Akron, Ohio   Mason City, Iowa

SERVICES
Willim Funeral Home
Clarion, Iowa
10:00 A.M. - October 24, 1997

WORDS OF COMFORT
Rev. Gary Boen - First Lutheran Church
Rev. Pat Nemmers - Holmes Baptist Church

MUSIC
Gary Brandt
"How Great Thou Art" *"Wish You Were Here"*

HONORARY BEARERS

Alice Cooper	Michael Bruce
Dennis Dunaway	Randy Kirstein
Neal Smith	Ron Baas
Craig Radechel	

CASKET BEARERS

Robert Busick	John Stevenson
Michael Busick	Lenny Zacks
Ed Schmanke	Chris Grill

INTERMENT
Evergreen Cemetery
Clarion, Iowa

Lorrie's Star

Some stars burn out and are
lost on their way back to earth.
On Glens way back to earth,
Glen found an angel.
Glen held on to her.
She held on to him.
Lorrie's star will shine forever

You are invited for lunch at the Pizza Ranch
following the committal service.

136

guitarist we ever used. The Piney Woodstock show went great. I had a backing band that I had met up with in Loftin, Texas — it was a good crowd.

In Ocober 1997 Neal, Glen, Richie and myself attended a Houston Record convention where people were selling videos, CDs and bootlegs. We decided to make the most of the fact that we had got together and organised a show at Billy Blue's nightclub which they broadcast live on the *Stevens and Prewett* radio show. We also did a gig at the Area 51 club in Houston.

It was the first time I had met Glen in over 15 years and it was good to see him. He seemed to be in good shape or at least better than I could have imagined — and still playing guitar! He was still drinking some beers and smoking cigarettes, but he was much more together than I expected. His playing was good but sometimes rambling — but still much better than the last time I remember seeing him play. We still had to be real patient with him and take a lot of time and go over things. He wasn't as fast as he used to be, we'd work out something and the next day he'd come to rehearsal and have forgotten it. So it was a bit frustrating. But he was still struggling. I don't think he was ever able to get over some of the things he had done. I remember him jokingly saying, "If I'd have known I was going to live this long I wouldn't have done all those things!"

The radio broadcast at Billy Blue's was recorded live in front of an audience at 7:30 in the morning for KLOL radio Houston — a Texas simulcast to 200,000 people. Glen had stayed at Jeff's house so he could be woken up a few hours early to get ready — I think he gave him lots of coffee. The show went real well even though Neal in his typical easy going way didn't really want to do a lot of songs for the gig. In the end I think Neal enjoyed it a lot. I'm glad we had the opportunity to play as much as we did with Glen.

We played "Schools Out", "No More Mr. Nice Guy", "Billion Dollar Babies", "I'm Eighteen", "Be My Lover", and "Muscle Of Love". That was on the Friday morning and on the Sunday evening we did the show at the Area 51 club which was packed! We also did a publicity photo shoot with motorcycles and some girls — now known as the 'Bikes & Babes' photo shoot. It was a great weekend.

There was a memorable incident when we all went to this Chinese restaurant one night. Richie Scarlet hates seafood or anything from the sea. So when Glen ordered this whole big Bass and the waiter brings it out and sets it right down in front of Richie — well he almost pukes. He just about got sick looking at this thing. It was really awful smelling and looked all blue. And Glen's eating this fish and he picks the eyeball out and ate it — that might have been the thing that killed him, I don't know. In any event, Glen returned to Iowa right after the Area 51 show and there was some talk of a longer lasting reunion. Neal was even talking about getting Alice involved — something he had been trying to work on for what seemed like forever. But the question was still — "how are we going to deal with Glen". He wouldn't have been able to go on the road, or put himself through any gruelling sort of situation. As it turned out the full Alice Cooper group reunion never happened.

Whilst in Houston Glen had evidently picked up some sort of flu bug — the air in Houston is real moist and there are a lot of microbes and what not floating around. Glen's flu developed into a respiratory illness and eventually into pneumonia which effected his heart and proved fatal. I found out later from his fiancé that he should have had a flu shot, but in typical fashion he hadn't. The doctor had already told him point blank that if he got the flu or pneumonia it would probably kill him. I guess the years of abuse to his system left him weak and susceptible — his body couldn't fight it. It's sad to think that a simple flu shot could probably have saved his life. But Glen was real stubborn — some people don't like to go to doctors I guess. He passed away on the morning of October 18th, 1997.

It was my manager who called me and told me the sad news. I then called Dennis and Ant-Bee, who in turn phoned Brian Nelson who alerted Alice. It was really shocking because we had just spent about a month with Glen, and one minute he seemed fine and then the next week he was gone. But, at the risk of sounding harsh, it was surprising to me that he hadn't died sooner.

The funeral was really touching — the whole town turned out. Evidently Glen had been in Clarion for quite a while and I guess he had affected the whole town. Across the board Glen was very well liked. It was good to see that a bunch of different people from all walks of life attended his funeral. Alice unfortunately couldn't make it. I wish he could have, but life goes on and a lot of other people couldn't make it either. So I don't think it really meant anything — one way or another. Paul Brenton helped set up the memorial fund for a headstone for Glen and set aside a special day for him to be remembered. Originally everyone kicked around the idea of asking for donations to raise some money to buy a headstone. But ultimately the Glen Buxton Memorial was put together in Clarion the next year. And that's when they unveiled the headstone.

In November 1997, my website was created. I didn't really know what I wanted from the site, so I started looking around at other sites to get ideas. I really liked Jan Akkerman's website (the Dutch guitarist from Focus) — it is really elaborate, so I guess compared to that my site still has a long way to go, but at least people can check out my history, recent activities and tour dates. People from Europe that I otherwise wouldn't have much contact with are dropping me e-mails. It has also helped me (and Neal I'm sure) to see that we still have a lot of fans out there that still care about what we're doing. Also my site has helped me get in touch with a lot of people from my past. I'm looking forward to putting some soundbites of some of my new material on the site at some point in the future.

In early 1998, I formed a new Michael Bruce Group and played the Cardi's club in Texas which was filmed, as well as touring through the US from May to August. The band was Will Hutchins on bass, Troy Powell on drums, Dave Mostravito on guitar and John Glen on keyboards. We did all the old classic Cooper stuff plus "Rock Rolls On" and "Left For Dead Meat." The tour allowed me to get back into the groove again — there weren't big crowds but the response was great! Unfortunately, the promotion was really lacking. Booking agents are very hesitant about laying out the cash to promote small gigs in fear of not getting a return from the ticket sales.

In August 1998, Dennis, Neal, Rockin' Reggie and myself attended the Glen Buxton Memorial Weekend in Clarion, Iowa. A stripped down version of my group (we had lost Dave the keyboardist and John the guitarist at this point) played at a club called Little Willie. Neal was there and so was Dennis but they didn't perform at this event. I did the show as a trio with Will and Troy. But pretty much the pinnacle of this event was the unveiling of Glen's headstone. That was the whole thing everyone had worked towards purchasing.

Around this time I received a Gibson guitar endorsement and once again headlined the Piney Woodstock show with Rick Derringer. It was a great time — a couple thousand people were there. Rick and I hung out a bit — we went back to his hotel and he had his lap top computer there and he was putting pictures from the show straight onto his website.

In October 1998, I attended the Chiller Convention in NJ, with Neal, Dennis and Richie. The Chiller Conventions are basically events where they sell a lot of movie, sci-fi and music memorabilia. A lot of rock 'n' rollers, actors, playmates, models turn up— it's a kind of entertainment biz gathering. They descend upon New Jersey two times a year and have a blast! I performed as well as signed autographs and sold books. Neal and Richie sat in with my group which was fun! Also, Cherry from the Runnaways got up and sang a number with us. We were the only group that played — other than the promotor, who had a band.

On December 19th, 1998, Alice opened his restaurant in Arizona called Cooperstown. I heard that Neal was going to the launch, so I took the opportunity to go out there as well and check the scene out. As it happened they also had a stage set up, so I took my guitar. Sure enough, Neal and I got up there with Alice and did five or six songs. We played "Under My Wheels", "Schools Out", "Muscle Of Love", "Desperado", "No More Mr. Nice Guy". On "Billion Dollar Babies" Rockin' Reggie got up and sang with us. It was the first time we had performed together since the Alice Cooper group break-up. It felt like we'd been playing together all along.

More than any one event, I think this was a turning point in my relationship with Alice. I think it healed a few wounds. I'm not sure when the last time Alice had played with Neal, but he hadn't played with me in nearly 25 years! I think he really wasn't sure if I could play anymore. I think this proved to him I still could. It was a pretty amazing, magical night! Everybody had fun.

1999 saw two significant releases. Firstly there was the VH1 TV special *Behind The Music*, and secondly the CD Box set called *Life and Crimes of Alice Cooper*.

The VH1 special was kind of a bittersweet experience. I know Alice is the namesake of the band and a lot has been written and said about him as a solo artist. Therefore, it was understandable that quite a bit of the show was taken up with the problems he'd had in the past — drinking and so forth. But unfortunately they cut out the part about Glen's passing away, which was very

Opposite top: Onstage with Alice's band at Cooperstown, December 1998.
Middle: Neal, Alice and Myself in the Cooperstown kitchen.
Bottom: Alice meets and greets a lookalike fan.
Photos: Jeff Jatras, Bill Risoli, Brian Nelson

disappointing to all of us — and I'm sure Alice too. Although it was fairly limited, it was a good opportunity to let people know I was still around and to see my face again. Actually Billy James' friend David Tedds knew the producer of the show, and that's how I was contacted to do it.

As for the box-set — overall I liked it. I think you have to be a fan of the group and Alice's solo career to really like the whole thing. I'm glad they included a track from the Billion Dollar Babies *Battle Axe* album. But after that the box departs from the group and goes on to Alice's solo career. I think they did a real good job. From what I heard the sales have been good. I heard that they pressed 60,000 units. Also I understand they're going to do deluxe remasters of *Billion Dollar Babies* and *School's Out*.

In July 1999, I went back to North Carolina to record the lead vocals for two tracks on the Bruce Cameron *Midnight Daydream* CD. I had first met Bruce back in 1996 when my bass player, Ronnie Newman, took me over to Bruce's house. He was a real nice guy and a big fan of the Cooper group. He played me some of his music and I could tell he was very talented and a good guitarist.

So, when Ant-Bee contacted me about contributing to Bruce's new CD project, I looked forward to doing vocals on the two tracks he was recording ("Falling Up A Mountain" and "I Want To Be Late"). Neal played drums on both tracks. I could see where he was going with the songs — he wanted a Cooper/Sabbath/Marilyn Manson dark type of feel to them, whilst also sounding like some of the newer alternative stuff.

The CD also features Neal Smith, Jack Bruce (Cream), Mitch Mitchell (Jimi Hendrix Experience), Buddy Miles & Billy Cox (Band of Gypsies), Ken Hensley (Uriah Heep), Bunk Gardner (Mothers), Harvey Dalton Arnold (Outlaws) and Ant-Bee (who served as the project co-ordinator). Sadly Bruce Cameron committed suicide on October 16th, 1999 just one month after the CD was released.

I was very saddened by the news of his death. It's a shame we couldn't have seen it coming and helped him. He seemed totally together when we were recording the songs. In some ways, I almost feel like he orchestrated the whole thing — there's a part of me that says this guy knew just what he wanted and he decided to go out in a blaze of glory. I think he wanted to play with his musical heroes and he got the chance to do an album with them. The album is great but I'm not sure how it will do. Either it will take off and be a classic

Above: Myself, the legendary Les Paul and Phil from Monstermagnet.
Photo: George Orlay

Below: Joining the literary elite, with Anne Rice, author of *Interview With The Vampire*
at the Big Easy Comic Convention, May 2000. *Photo: Kevin Londreneau*

Above: Bruce Cameron, Myself and Ant-Bee in July 1999 during the record-
ing of Midnight Daydream. *Photo: Andy Long.*
Below: Me and my children, 1999, Tyler and Chandler and Mikaela.
Photo: Paul Duffy

or just fade away. Let's hope it's the former.

During October 1999, I played twice on stage with Alice. Firstly, he was playing two shows at the Trump Marina and the first night I went backstage and said, "Hi". Alice asked me what I was doing, and I said, "Well, I'm here but I wasn't planning on seeing the show." So he said, "Come on down and play on 'Under My Wheels'!" I said, "Great!" I had my guitar with me. There was around 3 or 4 thousand people there and the response when I came on stage was great — a lot of yelling and screaming! But I wasn't really paying attention it happened so fast. I took the intro and outro solos — it was almost like being Rick Derringer playing along with the Cooper band when they first started.

Secondly, Alice, Dennis, Neal and myself played the second annual Glen Buxton Memorial Weekend which took place at Cooperstown in Phoenix. It was the first time all the surviving members had performed together in 25 years!

Dennis's playing was great — he wasn't jumping around as much as he used to, but he looked and sounded good. Over the years, I often think that Dennis has fared the best of all. He's still happily married to Cindy and has two wonderful daughters. He runs a chain of video stores and he continues to do things he likes. As it turns out, his lethargic nature was the result of really low blood pressure and that's why he got into a real strict vegetarian diet, and why he didn't smoke and rarely drank. I can't think of anyone who didn't like Dennis. Once you got to know him he would really warm up to you.

The night after we played at Cooperstown, Neal and Dennis came over to my hotel, and my friend Mike Postal suggested we all go down to his rehearsal room. In the end, everybody left in the hotel came with us and there must have been 40 people crowded into this little rehearsal room. We did some of the old material and some people got up and sang with us on songs like "The Ballad Of Dwight Frye" — it was really wild. Someone shot a video of the whole session, so who knows?

As for the future, I'm determined to get a damn album out finally! I never really got *In My Own Way* released properly back then — so this time I'm going to push on forward. I have some new material and I would like to put together a new Michael Bruce Group to tour in some form or another. I would very much like to tour Europe, Australia and Japan. I would also like to do something with Dennis and Neal again — a rep from Sony suggested us doing a live album of the old stuff. But I still want to get a new solo album out first.

As for the perennial question as to whether the original band will ever tour again. Neal in particular has remained friends with Alice over the years. Although Neal is now a very successful real estate agent in Westport, I think he has always held the hope that Alice and the original band would get back together again some day. Over the years there have been a number of false starts. I remember a few years back, Neal came out to Phoenix and he and Alice played golf and Alice apparently said, "Sure I'll sing on a song with you guys". We had a song written for him to sing, but again Warner Bros weren't interested in the project and neither was Shep. This may sound egotistical, but if we got together with Alice and tried to write some new material like we did in the old days, I think we could come up with some great songs! I also think if somebody approached Alice with the right material and a concept that he could write and work within, it could happen.

A lot of time has certainly elapsed and Alice has done a lot of the old material over the years with other musicians. A couple people have suggested a 27-year anniversary tour of the *Billion Dollar Babies* show which was the number 1 tour in 1973! I think a lot of people would come because there must be a lot of kids who have heard about the original group but were too young to have seen us. I think that it would work if we did some major shows on the East coast and Europe — places where the band were strong. Hey, I'd be up for trying it — I know Dennis and Neal would be too!

Above: The reunion at Cooperstown. (l-r) Dennis Dunaway, Myself, Alice, Rockin' Reggie Vincent, and Neal Smith.
Photo: Bill Risoli

Left: Alice and myself at Trump Casino, Atlantic City, New Jersey, 1999.
Photo: Mich Barnes.

Discography

THE BEST OF MICHAEL BRUCE

Discography

THE WILD FLOWERS
On A Day Like Today b/w A Man Like Myself (Aster A-WF-1/2)
More Than Me b/w Moving Along With The Sun (Aster A-WF-3/4)

THE SPIDERS
Don't Blow Your Mind b/w No Price Tag (Santa Cruz SCR 10.003)

THE NAZZ
Wonder Who's Loving Her Now b/w Lay Down And Die, Goodbye (Very 001)

THE ALICE COOPER GROUP

PRETTIES FOR YOU
Straight STS 1051
Released: December 1969
Produced: by the Alice Cooper group
Titanic Overture - 10 Minutes before the Worm - Sing Low, Sweet Cheerio - Today Mueller - Living - Fields of Regret - No Longer Umpire - Levity Ball - B.B. on Mars - Reflected - Apple Bush - Earwigs to Eternity - Changing, Arranging

EASY ACTION
Straight STS 1061
Released: June 1970
Produced by David Briggs
Mr. and Misdemeanor - Shoe Salesman - Still No Air - Below Your Means -
Return of the Spiders - Laughing at Me - Refrigerator Heaven
Beautiful Flyaway - Lay Down and Die, Goodbye

LOVE IT TO DEATH
Straight STS 1065 Warner Bros. WS 1883
Released June 1971
Produced by Jack Richardson and Bob Ezrin
Re-released in December 1971 on Warner Bros.
(UK: K46177, US: WS 1883)
Caught in a Dream - I'm Eighteen - Long Way to Go - Black Ju Ju - Is It My
Body - Hallowed Be My Name - Second Coming - Ballad of Dwightt Frye -
Sun Arise
(A live version of "Black Ju Ju" appeared on the *Great Medicine Ball Caravan*
soundtrack album.)

KILLER
Warner Bros. (UK: K56005, US:BS 2567)
Released in November 1971 (initial copies included calendar)
Produced by Bob Fzrin
Under My Wheels - Be My Lover - Halo of Flies - Desperado - You Drive Me
Nervous - Yeah, Yeah, Yeah - Dead Babies - Killer

SCHOOL'S OUT
Warner Bros. (US: BS 2623, UK: K56007)
Released in June 1972
Produced by Bob Ezrin
School's Out - Luney Tune - Gutter Cat vs. the Jets - Street Fight - Blue Turk -
My Stars - Public Animal No.9 - Alma Mater - Grande Finale

Billion Dollar Babies
Warner Bros. (US: BS 2685, UK: K56013)
Released in March 1973
Produced by Bob Ezrin
Hello Hooray - Raped and Freezin' - Elected - Billion Dollar Babies - Unfinished Sweet - No More Mr. Nice Guy - Generation Landslide - Sick Things - Mary Ann - I Love the Dead

Muscle Of Love
Warner Bros. (US: BS 2748, UK56018)
Released in December 1973
Produced by Jack Richardson
Muscle of Love - Woman Machine - Hard Hearted Alice - Man with the Gold Gun - Big Apple Dreamin' (Hippo) - Never Been Sold Before - Working Up a Sweat - Crazy Little Child - Teenage Lament '74

Alice Cooper's Greatest Hits
Warner Bros. (US: W 2803, UKK56043)
Released in August 1974
I'm Eighteen - Is It My Body - Desperado - Under My Wheels - Be My Lover - School's Out - Hello Hooray - Elected - No More Mr. Nice Guy - Billion Dollar Babies - Teenage Lament '74 - Muscle of Love

Billion Dollar Babies

Battle Axe
Polydor (US: PD-1-6100)
Released in 1977
Too Young - Shine Your Love - I Miss You - Wasn't I The One - Love Is Rather Blind - Rock 'n' Roll Radio - Dance With Me - Rock Me Slowly - Ego Mania - Battle Axe/ Sudden Death - Winner

MICHAEL BRUCE

IN MY OWN WAY
Polydor (1975) New reissue on One Way Records (early 1997)
King Of America - Lucky Break - Friday On My Mind - In My Own Way - As
Rock Rolls On - If The Sky Should Fall - So Far So Good - Got To Get Hold
Of Myself - Seems Like I'm Only Fooling Myself - Morning Song

ROCK ROLLS ON
Euro Tec Records (1983)
Rock Rolls On - Gina - Too Young - Friday On My Mind - Lucky Break - In
My Own Way - Do You Wanna Know

Titles available from SAF, Firefly and Helter Skelter Publishing

NO MORE MR NICE GUY: THE INSIDE STORY OF THE ALICE COOPER GROUP
By Michael Bruce and Billy James UK Price £11.99
The dead babies, the drinking, executions and, of course, the rock 'n' roll.

PROCOL HARUM: BEYOND THE PALE
by Claes Johansen UK Price £12.99
Distinctive, ground breaking and enigmatic British band from the 60s.

AN AMERICAN BAND: THE STORY OF GRAND FUNK RAILROAD
By Billy James UK Price £12.99
One of the biggest grossing US rock 'n' roll acts of the 70s - selling millions of records and playing sold out arenas the world over. Hype, Politics & rock 'n' roll - unbeatable!

WISH THE WORLD AWAY: MARK EITZEL AND AMERICAN MUSIC CLUB
by Sean Body UK Price £12.99
Sean Body has written a fascinating biography of Eitzel which portrays an artist tortured by demons, yet redeemed by the aching beauty of his songs.

GINGER GEEZER: VIVIAN STANSHALL AND THE BONZO DOG BAND
by Chris Welch and Lucian Randall UK Price £12.99 (available soon)
Stanshall was one of pop music's true eccentrics. An account of his incredible life from playing pranks with The Who's Keith Moon to depression, alcoholism, & sad demise.

GO AHEAD JOHN! THE MUSIC OF JOHN MCLAUGHLIN
by Paul Stump UK Price £12.99
One of the greatest jazz musicians of all time. Includes his work with Miles Davis, Mahavishnu Orchestra, Shakti. Full of insights into all stages of his career.

LUNAR NOTES: ZOOT HORN ROLLO'S CAPTAIN BEEFHEART EXPERIENCE
by Bill Harkleroad and Billy James UK Price £11.95
For the first time we get the insider's story of what it was like to record, play and live with an eccentric genius such as Beefheart, written by Bill Harkleroad - Zoot himself!

MEET THE RESIDENTS: AMERICA'S MOST ECCENTRIC BAND
by Ian Shirley UK Price £11.95
An outsider's view of The Residents' operations, exposing a world where nothing is as it seems. It is a fascinating tale of musical anarchy and cartoon wackiness. Reprinted to coincide with the recent world tour.

DIGITAL GOTHIC: A CRITICAL DISCOGRAPHY OF TANGERINE DREAM
by Paul Stump UK Price £9.95
For the very first time German electronic pioneers, Tangerine Dream mammoth output is placed within an ordered perspective.

THE ONE AND ONLY - HOMME FATALE: PETER PERRETT & THE ONLY ONES
by Nina Antonia UK Price £11.95
An extraordinary journey through crime, punishment and the decadent times of British punk band leader, Peter Perrett of The Only Ones

PLUNDERPHONICS, 'PATAPHYSICS AND POP MECHANICS
The Leading Exponents of Musique Actuelle
By Andrew Jones UK Price £12.95
Chris Cutler, Fred Frith, Henry Threadgill, John Oswald, John Zorn, etc.

KRAFTWERK: MAN, MACHINE AND MUSIC
By Pascal Bussy UK Price £11.95
The full story behind one of the most influential bands in the history of rock.

WRONG MOVEMENTS: A ROBERT WYATT HISTORY
by Mike King UK Price £14.95
A journey through Wyatt's 30 year career with Soft Machine, Matching Mole & solo artist.

WIRE: EVERYBODY LOVES A HISTORY
by Kevin Eden UK Price £9.95
British punk's most endearing and enduring bands combining Art and Attitude

TAPE DELAY: A DOCUMENTARY OF INDUSTRIAL MUSIC
by Charles Neal
Marc Almond, Cabaret Voltaire, Nick Cave, Chris & Cosey, Coil, Foetus, Neubauten, Non, The Fall, New Order, Psychic TV, Rollins, Sonic Youth, Swans, Test Dept and many more...

DARK ENTRIES: BAUHAUS AND BEYOND
by Ian Shirley UK Price £11.95
The gothic rise of Bauhaus, Love & Rockets, Tones on Tail, Murphy, J, and Ash solo.

POISON HEART: SURVIVING THE RAMONES
by Dee Dee Ramone and Veronica KofmanUK Price £11.95
Dee Dee's crushingly honest account of life as junkie and Ramone. A great rock story!

MINSTRELS IN THE GALLERY: A HISTORY OF JETHRO TULL
by David Rees UK Price £12.99
At Last! To coincide with their 30th anniversary, a full history of one of the most popular and inventive bands of the past three decades

DANCEMUSICSEXROMANCE: PRINCE - THE FIRST DECADE
by Per Nilsen UK Price £12.99
A portrait of Prince's reign as the most exciting black performer to emerge since James Brown and Jimi Hendrix.

SOUL SACRIFICE: THE SANTANA STORY
by Simon Leng UK Price £12.99
In depth study of seventies Latin guitar legend whose career began at Woodstock through to a 1999 number one US album.

OPENING THE MUSICAL BOX: A GENESIS CHRONICLE
by Alan Hewitt UK Price £12.99
Drawing on hours of new interviews and packed with insights, anecdotes and trivia, here is the ultimat compendium to one of the most successful and inventive bands of the modern rock era.

WAITING FOR THE MAN: THE STORY OF DRUGS AND POPULAR MUSIC
by Harry Shapiro UK Price £12.99
Fully revised edition of the classic story of two intertwining billion dollar industries. "Wise and witty." The Guardian

THE SHARPER WORD: A MOD READER
Edited by Paolo Hewitt (available November 1999) UK price:£12.99
Hugely readable collection of articles documenting one of the most misunderstood cultural movements

DYLAN'S DAEMON LOVER: THE TANGLED TALE OF A 450-YEAR OLD POP BALLAD
by Clinton Heylin UK price £12.00
Written as a detective story, Heylin unearths the mystery of why Dylan knew enough to return "The House Carpenter" to its 16th century source.

GET BACK: THE BEATLES' LET IT BE DISASTER
by Doug Sulpy & Ray Schweighardt UK price £12.99
No-holds barred account of the power struggles, the bickering, and the bitterness that led to the break-up of the greatest band in the history of rock 'n' roll. "One of the most poignant Beatles books ever." Mojo

XTC: SONG STORIES - THE EXCLUSIVE & AUTHORISED STORY
by XTC and Neville Farmer UK Price £12.99
"A cheerful celebration of the minutiae surrounding XTC's music with the band's musical passion intact … high in setting-the-record-straight anecdotes. Superbright, funny, commanding." Mojo

LIKE THE NIGHT: BOB DYLAN AND THE ROAD TO THE MANCHESTER FREE TRADE HALL

by CP Lee UK Price £12.00

In 1966 at the height of Dylan's protest-singing popularity he plugged in an electric guitar to the outrage of folk fans who booed and jeered. Finally, in Manchester, fans branded him Judas. "Essential Reading" Uncut

BORN IN THE USA: BRUCE SPRINGSTEEN AND THE AMERICAN TRADITION

by Jim Cullen UK Price £9.99

"Cullen has written an excellent treatise expressing exactly how and why Springsteen translated his uneducated hicktown American-ness into music and stories that touched hearts and souls around the world." Q****

BACK TO THE BEACH: A BRIAN WILSON AND THE BEACH BOYS READER

Ed Kingsley Abbott UK Price £12.99

"A detailed study and comprehensive overview of the BBs' lives and music, even including a foreword from Wilson himself by way of validation. Most impressively, Abbott manages to appeal to both die-hard fans and rather less obsessive newcomers." Time Out   "Rivetting!" **** Q "An essential purchase." Mojo

A JOURNEY THROUGH AMERICA WITH THE ROLLING STONES

by Robert Greenfield UK Price £12.00

This is the definitive account of their legendary '72 tour.

"Filled with finely-rendered detail ... a fascinating tale of times we shall never see again" Mojo

BOB DYLAN

by Anthony Scaduto UK Price £12.99

The first and best biography of Dylan. "The best book ever written on Dylan" Record Collector "Now in a welcome reprint it's a real treat to read the still-classic Bobography". Q*****

MAIL ORDER

All Firefly, SAF and Helter Skelter titles are available by mail order from the world famous Helter Skelter bookshop.

You can either phone or fax your order to Helter Skelter on the following numbers:

Telephone: +44 (0)20 7836 1151 or Fax: +44 (0)20 7240 9880
Office hours: Mon-Fri 10:00am - 7:00pm, Sat: 10:00am - 6:00pm, Sun: closed.

Postage prices per book worldwide are as follows:

UK & Channel Islands	£1.50
Europe & Eire (air)	£2.95
USA, Canada (air)	£7.50
Australasia, Far East (air)	£9.00
Overseas (surface)	£2.50

You can also write enclosing a cheque, International Money Order, or registered cash. Please include postage. DO NOT send cash. DO NOT send foreign currency, or cheques drawn on an overseas bank. Send to:

**Helter Skelter Bookshop,
4 Denmark Street, London, WC2H 8LL, United Kingdom.**
If you are in London come and visit us, and browse the titles in person!!

**Email: helter@skelter.demon.co.uk
Website: http://www.skelter.demon.co.uk**

For the latest on SAF and Firefly titles check the SAF website:
www.safpublishing.com

SAF Publishing Ltd

www.safpublishing.com